"Reflects the hardships, f
bewilderment of living .

-**Larry Brown**, CEO, E<small>THNOS</small>360*

"*An entertaining and informative jungle adventure. Two thumbs up!*"

-**Gracia Burnham**, A<small>UTHOR</small> O<small>F</small> I<small>N</small> T<small>HE</small> P<small>RESENCE</small> O<small>F</small> M<small>Y</small> E<small>NEMIES</small>*

"*Davey and Marie demonstrate a transparency that is refreshing and appealing. Their message is riveting, engaging, humorous, and poignant.*"

-**Mike Calhoun, S<small>R</small>**. V<small>ICE</small>-P<small>RESIDENT</small>, W<small>ORD</small> O<small>F</small> L<small>IFE</small> F<small>ELLOWSHIP</small>*

"*When Davey and Marie write about the jungle, you can smell it.*"

-**John R Cross**, A<small>UTHOR</small> A<small>ND</small> T<small>EACHER</small>, G<small>OODSEED</small> I<small>NTERNATIONAL</small>*

"*These funny educational stories transport you to a world that few people experience.*"

-**Dr. Jack Eggar,** P<small>RESIDENT</small>/CEO, A<small>WANA</small>*

"*A delightful and challenging read that will be a great contribution to the annals of mission classics.*"

-**Dr. Don Fanning,** D<small>IRECTOR</small>, C<small>ENTER</small> F<small>OR</small> G<small>LOBAL</small> M<small>INISTRIES</small>, L<small>IBERTY</small> U<small>NIVERSITY</small>*

"*This book takes you along the jungle trails. I couldn't put it down until I finished reading the final chapter.*"

-**Dr. Roy Lawson,** F<small>ELLOWSHIP</small> O<small>F</small> E<small>VANGELICAL</small> B<small>APTIST</small> C<small>HURCHES</small> C<small>ANADA</small>*

"*Davey and Marie write from inside the culture of the Wilo people of the Amazon jungle. By turns humorous, touching, heartbreaking, and very readable.*"

-**Dr. Michael Pocock**, S<small>ENIOR</small> P<small>ROFESSOR</small> A<small>ND</small> C<small>HAIRMAN</small>, W<small>ORLD</small> M<small>ISSIONS</small> A<small>ND</small> I<small>NTERCULTURAL</small> S<small>TUDIES</small>, D<small>ALLAS</small> T<small>HEOLOGICAL</small> S<small>EMINARY</small>*

*Endorsement given while titled Our Witchdoctors Are Too Weak

PIRANHA LAST LINE is an imprint of LAST LINE PUBLISHING

Inquiries may be directed to:
info@lastlinepublishing.com
www.lastlinepublishing.com

2nd EDITION

ISBN-13: 978-1-947777-00-2 (previously ISBN 978-0-85721-008- 1)
ISBN-10: 1-947777-00-9

Cover design by: Micah Jank
micahjank@gmail.com

MESSENGER IN A BOTTLE

Davey & Marie Jank

PIRANHA LAST LINE

Formerly published by Monarch Books,
an imprint of Lion Hudson plc, under the title:
Our Witchdoctors Are Too Weak

No one seems to know exactly how it came about, but at some point the Wilo tribe developed an intense thirst for one particular book – a book that none of them could read nor understand, a book they referred to simply as "God's Talk." Their steadfast determination in this spiritual quest is what brought us into their jungle orbit, and their immeasurable patience toward us is what allowed them to finally obtain what they had so long been desiring: the Bible in their own language. We dedicate this book to the Wilo tribe. Otiwa!

Contents

Acknowledgments

Our experience in missions has been: people helping people help people. We're so thankful for the many sacrifices others have made over the years to facilitate our part in helping the Wilo people.

We're thankful also for the lives of our co-workers in the jungle who woke up every morning to quietly be about the business of succoring the needy and reaching out to the less fortunate, not to mention their ministry to the Wilo people as well.

Introduction

This Missionary

Why is this missionary hiding from the tribal people?

There's this missionary I know; your typical Bible-totin', pencil-chompin', coffee-chuggin' missionary. On a good day he is possessed of average looks, average talents, and average intellect; an unremarkable run-of-the-mill kind of person. Sometimes, though, he suspects he maybe isn't so typical. When people tell him, "Wow! I bet you really love those tribal people!" he wonders what odds they might be willing to offer. Love the tribal people? Well, maybe off and on. If he can love them on his own terms then yeah, maybe.

He certainly loves giving them the chance to hear and understand God's Word in their own language, but all too often he doesn't really want to get inserted into their lives too deeply. Sometimes he avoids them, complains about them, wishes he were somewhere else, and then goes about preparing Bible lessons that teach that God is love. Yuck! What kind of a missionary is that? That's what I want to know.

"But surely," you protest, "surely this missionary friend of yours isn't all that bad. After all, he was willing to leave his own family and friends and country, and go off to live in the jungle to help those tribal people."

To address that, allow me to recount an experience this missionary had. After a day's work, he had just settled into his office to enjoy a good book when he heard the murmur of approaching voices. He held his breath, hoping the tribal people would pass by, but no such luck. They came to the door and called his name, and he chose not to answer. Maybe they would conclude he was away. They called several more times, insistently, and then made their way around the mud-and-thatch house to the office window.

The missionary silently rose from the hammock and furtively eased out of the office, sidling into the adjoining bedroom. The would-be visitors looked in the office window and called out his name a few more times, frustration mounting in their voices.

Why were they being so persistent? Could it be they had seen me enter... I mean, seen the missionary enter into his house? Did they know he was there? The missionary remained silent, scarcely daring to breathe.

And then one of the determined visitors started slowly toward the bedroom window, effectively cornering the missionary. The situation was getting desperate. There was little recourse. It would be distasteful, but the missionary knew exactly what had to be done.

Drawing a deep breath, he frantically launched himself across the room, coming to rest beneath the window. A shadow fell across the floor as the caller loomed up at the window, but even though mere inches separated this missionary from the tribal man, he was safely out of the line of sight, safe from the embarrassment of being discovered. He wasn't about to be outmaneuvered at this point.

Pressed up against the cold mud wall, hiding from the people he was there to serve, this missionary realized he had not only succeeded in remaining undetected, but he had also succeeded in being both ridiculous and selfish in the process.

And what of the woman God gave this missionary? Why was she discovered one day hunkered down under the kitchen sink while several cute village children peered through the window, persistently calling her name? Could it be something in the drinking water?

Such are these missionaries. What is God to do with people like these? Beats me. But I suspect that God is OK with it – at least he isn't too surprised at their shortcomings. After all, God is great, and these missionaries aren't. God has always loved the Wilo people, and these missionaries haven't. God sees the whole picture while these missionaries obsess only with their own small space in it.

Thankfully, God is big enough to use people like these missionaries. He seems to enjoy taking human weakness and using it to bring honor and glory to himself. In that regard, this missionary was the perfect candidate.

Chapter 1

"No" is Not an Option

Going wild-pig hunting because I just couldn't say no

A group of people, some armed with shotguns, stampeded past my window, kicking up a cloud of dust in the dry-season heat. I stepped outside and waylaid a straggler.

"Hey! Where are you going?" I asked.

He screeched to a halt and hurriedly explained something about firewood.

"Firewood?" I asked. I had no idea why so many people would get this excited about firewood. Maybe there was a firewood clearance sale going on, which would explain the rush, and the shotguns.

Impatiently, like a child dancing on his tiptoes while desperately awaiting his turn at the bathroom, the straggler said, in Spanish, "Wild pigs!" Then he repeated the word in Wilo, which still sounded a lot like "firewood" to me.

"Do you want to come?" he asked, probably just wanting to end the conversation and catch up to the main group. At least that's what I deduced from the vaguely disappointed expression that flitted across his face when I said yes.

He wasn't the only one disappointed; so was I. Galloping through the briars and brambles of a jungle that had suddenly come alive with wild pigs, frantic dogs, shotguns, tribal hunters, and overall chaos wasn't very appealing to me on this fine day.

So why didn't I just say no? I would have liked to, but the Wilos just wouldn't take no for an answer. More accurately, I didn't know how to say "no" in their language. This was a substantial frustration to me. Saying "yes" was very easy; *ha-oh* was one of the first words I had learned in Wilo. But search though I might, I hadn't been able to find a word for "no".

The Spanish word for "no" is no. That's pretty simple. Why was the Wilo language being so difficult? I had even asked some of the Wilos who spoke a bit of Spanish how to say no in their language. They had given it some thought and then, somewhat perplexed, admitted they didn't know.

They didn't know? How could they not know? There's "yes", and there's "no". You can't have one without the other. It's not fair to not have a word for "no".

These were my thoughts as I galloped through the briars and brambles. We weren't seeing any wild pigs, but there was plenty of adrenaline-inducing activity nonetheless, such as when we slammed into a low-hanging bees' nest and then frantically attempted to outrun their counter-offensive. And I was reminded I wasn't in Kansas anymore when one of the Wilos later brought my attention to something on the side of the trail, something I had almost stepped in.

"*Yawi idebawo,*" he informed me.

"Is that right?" I said. That's just great. I knew that *yawi* was the word for "jaguar"; looking down, I could guess what *idebawo* might mean. Call me crazy, but I'm of the opinion that the only kinds of *idebawo* a person should have to avoid getting on their shoe are the pigeon or dog varieties. If stepping in jaguar *idebawo* is a hazard in your life, then you probably took a wrong turn somewhere.

The wild pigs stayed away, but so did the *yawi*, so I wasn't too disappointed. It wouldn't be until much later, after months of investigative language learning, that our missionary team would finally be convinced that in fact the Wilo language really did not have a word for "no". There was, however, a way to communicate the idea of "not". This was done by putting a negation suffix on the word in question, as well as conjugating it with a pronoun and verb tense. That's how the Wilos say "no".

I found it rather cumbersome to use initially, because it

required the ability to put together small sentences. For instance, when someone would ask, "Dah-wee, are you studying?" I had to respond with, "I'm studying-not." "Dah-wee, are you eating?" "I'm eating-not." "Dah-wee, do you want to go hunt wild pigs?" "Wild pig hunting I want to go-not." Now that would have been a practical thing to know how to say a few months earlier!

Chapter 2

The Snake Bite

An encounter with a venomous snake gives insight into tribal culture

I studied French when I was in junior high. Or maybe I should just say that I attended French class. It was pretty nice. Amenities included textbooks that provided invaluable help to those interested in actually learning, and study helps on audio cassette that we were able to listen to. The school library featured books that were geared toward helping people learn to speak French. We even had a teacher who spoke both French and English and was therefore able to correct us and instruct us in the proper pronunciation of words, and in charting the grammar. It was as though the red carpet of learning had been rolled out for us and servants lined the way, ready to attend to our every language-learning need.

That kind of red-carpet treatment was distressingly absent now. Where was I to begin learning a language that was completely unknown to the outside world? How was I to gain traction in this process when the language had no written form to it? To whom could I turn to learn the meaning of all the strange sounds I was hearing the Wilos speak? Much to my dismay, after conducting a little research, I reached the conclusion that the answer was not to be found in my hammock. Every day, I had to put on my shoes and go outside. My classroom awaited me.

On this particular morning, the ever-present gathering of children outside my house parted like the Red Sea as I stepped through the doorway into the glaring morning sunlight. It wasn't long ago that most of these little ones would have scattered at my exit, but now they remained nearby, though apprehensively watching my every move. When they saw that I was not going to morph into some terrible monster, and that my intent was to walk toward the nearby village houses, they boisterously fell in behind me.

Feeling uncomfortably like the Pied Piper, I arrived at the house of Odowiya and found him and Snail on the porch, talking about their plans for the day.

In the little time that I had known him, I could always count on Odowiya to be of good humor. He had a knack for making me feel comfortable by taking my blunders and ignorance in his stride.

This morning, I was distressed to see a different side of him. With a scowl on his face, and without so much as saying hello, he directed his gaze toward me and commenced a loud tirade. My heart skipped a beat. Had I unwittingly offended him? Was it rude to show up unannounced in the morning? Had I interrupted an important ritual?

I soon realized, much to my relief, that his gaze and words were not directed at me, but at my entourage. The children immediately retreated. I wondered if perhaps he had woken up on the wrong side of the hammock that morning, but as soon as his voice of reprimand ceased reverberating through the neighborhood, his expression immediately reverted back to its normal friendly self. Like most of the adults in the village, he tended to go out of his way to make sure that the children weren't pestering the newly arrived missionary.

If I had been more like Christ, perhaps I would have said, "Suffer the children to come unto me." Even had I been inclined to, I wouldn't have known how to say something like that, so I kept my mouth shut and sat down beside Odowiya. The scolded children hovered just outside the danger zone, pretending they had lost interest.

With an animated but confusing combination of Spanish and Wilo, illustrated with hand gestures, Odowiya told me that he and Snail were heading out to the jungle to cut down some poles for

Snail's new house. Did I want to come along?

"*Ha-oh*," I replied. I already knew from experience that Odowiya was a regular Energizer Bunny when it came to walking through the jungle, his bare feet nimbly propelling him over rocks and roots, across makeshift bridges and over fallen trees. I wasn't too excited about the prospect of being led on yet another death march by this man. Nevertheless, I took comfort in the tenuous assumption that someone named Snail would walk a little slower.

Several hours later, sweat beading my forehead, I still hadn't figured out why someone who walks so fast for so long would be named Snail. He was leading the way, with Odowiya and me walking single file behind him. The two of them were carrying on a lively discussion as we went along.

Listening carefully to them, I was pleased to note that the many long hours of language study were finally paying dividends: this kind of conversation no longer sounded like a flock of agitated ducks boisterously passing overhead. Now it sounded like a strange unintelligible language passing over my head. Progress, I thought morosely, comes in many different shapes, sizes, and flavors.

I nevertheless continued trying to catch a word or two of what they were saying. I was walking with notebook and pencil in hand, writing down any sounds I was able to hear clearly enough. The Wilo people had no alphabet for their language, so for the time being I wrote using a phonetic alphabet. Eventually our team would be able to develop an alphabet for the Wilo language, but we would have to progress much further in our understanding of the language before we could focus on that. For now, I was going generic.

Preoccupied with pencil and paper, I didn't notice when Snail and Odowiya pulled away from me, but when I looked up, they were gone. I hurried to the next bend in the trail, and to my relief they were standing together, waiting for me. They said something, pointing in the general vicinity of my feet.

It has been my experience that, in the jungle, rarely is it desirable to have anything of consequence on the trail near one's feet. I immediately braked my forward momentum and looked down. A cursory glance revealed nothing. I took a cautious step forward and that's when I saw what they were pointing at. Coiled up among the leaves that carpeted the trail was a venomous snake.

It didn't look upset. In fact, it looked like it was enjoying some morning shut-eye, which was fortunate for Snail and Odowiya; they had been so engrossed in their conversation that they had both stepped right over it. Odowiya though, had caught a glimpse of the snake as he passed over, so they had decided to wait for me to catch up so they could point it out to me and inform me that it was called *anko'da*. That was nice of them.

They told me that I should carefully step around it, which didn't sound like a very good idea to me; just looking at a snake gives me the heebie-jeebies. If a snake were going to kill me, I preferred that it not be because I was politely trying to not disturb its little nap.

When he saw my hesitation, Odowiya picked up a stick and with one deft stroke killed the snake. He squatted down beside it, and with his machete he cut off the tip of the tail. Flashing a mischievous smile, he then popped the severed portion into his mouth and swallowed it like a pill. He and Snail exchanged a chuckle and continued on down the trail.

I was perplexed by what had just transpired, but at the same time relieved on two counts: not only had the snake been removed from the trail, but Odowiya hadn't offered any of it to me.

It was disturbing, however, to realize how little I understood about what was happening around me. Why had they initially not wanted to kill the snake? Was it taboo to harm a snake that was not aggressive? Did they perhaps think the snake was an ancestor? A protector of the trail? What was the purpose in cutting off the tip of the tail and eating it? I didn't doubt there was significance to what Odowiya had done, but I had no idea what it might be.

Many months after that incident, armed with a better grasp of how to formulate questions in the Wilo language, I reminded Odowiya about it. "Why did you cut off the tail and swallow it?" I asked.

"It didn't bite me," he answered. "I ate the tail so that the next time I step close to a snake, that one won't bite me either."

Maybe I should have considered taking a bite out of that *anko'da*, myself.

Chapter 3

Abandoned by the Mother Ship

Surrounded by curious tribal people after being deposited at a remote jungle airstrip

Even though I was quite new to his village, Odowiya and I already had a meaningful history together. Just a few months earlier, he had come riding to my rescue in a manner that will no doubt stay with me the rest of my cognitive life. That was the day a missionary bush pilot named Roland had taken me from the comforts and conveniences of civilization, and had deposited me into the Amazon jungle. Thanks a lot, Roland. Go ahead, Roland. Just fly away and abandon me here at this isolated jungle airstrip. Go on home to your wife and kids, Roland, and leave me holding the bag, surrounded by a bunch of unknown faces in the middle of nowhere.

So that's what he had done. I no doubt presented a forlorn and lonely figure, standing in the tall grass watching the airplane roar past and lift up into the air, but that hadn't stopped Roland from merrily tipping his wings in salute as he circled once and began the one-hour flight back to town.

That day, I had finally come to understand what it must have felt like for the disciples of Jesus to watch him ascend into the sky. Even after the airplane had disappeared I couldn't pry my eyes away from the point where it had entered the clouds. Looking away would make me have to confront my new reality. Confronting my new reality would likely make me sick.

"Why stand ye there gazing?" one of the tribal men asked me. Or maybe that was just my imagination. In any case, I reluctantly lowered my gaze from heaven and looked at the silent throng of tribal people surrounding me. I didn't speak their language, and they didn't speak mine. I tried a tentative smile that felt more like a grimace, and a few of them hesitantly responded with an equally uncertain smile, never taking their gaze off me. I was the alien who had been abandoned by the mother ship. Nobody was sure what to do next. Everyone was a tad nervous and apprehensive.

"Take-me-to-your-leader," I would have said robotically, but I doubted they were very current with pop-culture humor. Instead, I adjusted the bag strapped over my shoulder, picked up as many other things as I could carry, and with another smile, staggered laboriously down the jungle trail toward the village. Behind me the silence was finally broken as relieved conversation washed over the gathering. They picked up what remained of my things, and together we made our way through the jungle until we emerged at the top of a hill overlooking Poleni village.

There were several dozen houses spread out below, some topped with tin, others with brown thatch. We started down the hill and into the village clearing, and from the houses, dozens of eyes warily marked my progress. Women and children stood in the safety of their doorways, staring out with anxious curiosity. Someone motioned for me to follow them into a dark, windowless house where one of the women was preparing a simple drink of water flavored with manioc.

Entering the house, I deposited my gear into a corner and perched myself on a precarious chair that was proffered by a hand that reached out from the darkness. I was very relieved to hear a shadowy figure greet me in Spanish. I had been led to the house of a government-employed teacher there in the village. A stream of curious Wilos quickly filled the one-room house until there was no more standing room, which only in small part explained the sweat that ran down my brow and stung my eyes.

Eventually, I was able to understand that most of the men of the village were gone and wouldn't get back for a week or so. There was nobody available to take me upriver to Pakali, which was my final destination.

Earlier that morning Roland and I had flown over Pakali village, but there was no airstrip there, so after circling once or twice and revving the engine, we had continued on downriver to Poleni where an airstrip had recently been made by the tribal people. I was holding out a tiny ray of hope that the people of Pakali were gifted in the art of osmosis and would conclude that I was in the airplane that had flown over their village and that I was in need of a ride. If so, they might send someone to come pick me up.

Otherwise, my options were few: I could go to the riverbank and stand there with my thumb out. Though passing natives wouldn't recognize the gesture as a request for a ride, they might assume I had injured my thumb and stop to help. Or I could just sit tight and see what developed.

After several hours of sitting tight and seeing nothing at all develop, we heard the welcome sound of an outboard motor approaching. A few children ducked out the doorway and ran down to the river to see who had arrived. Within a few short minutes they were back, excitedly talking and looking at me and motioning toward the river. My ride had arrived.

I still don't understand exactly how the people in Pakali concluded that I was in the airplane that had flown over their village that morning. I don't know how they guessed that I would need their assistance. Fortunately for me, they had connected all the dots, and someone had been dispatched to pick me up at Poleni. God was working things out just fine, and I was reminded that I could relax and let God handle the details, since he does that so well.

Once again everything I had brought with me was scooped up by the Wilos, and we made our way to the riverbank, where the dugout boat awaited me. When I got to the boat I saw that my welcoming committee was a young boy accompanied by a man with an open and friendly countenance. We shook hands a bit clumsily, since that is not the customary way for the Wilos to greet each other. Then we piled my supplies into the boat and pushed off from the bank.

I had no idea at the time, that the man driving the boat was to become one of my closest friends. I was unaware of our future, and I didn't even think to ask him his name; I was just glad to be on my way to Pakali, to the life and ministry that awaited me there. From here it would be a straight shot upriver; roughly a two-hour ride. God was good, and things would work out just fine. That was my mind-frame, and it would remain my mind-frame for almost an entire hour.

Everything was going great. It was a nice sunny day, with a pleasant breeze blowing across the river. I was enjoying the boat ride. But I began feeling a touch of concern when the boat abruptly turned off the main river and began winding its way up what appeared to be a small tributary.

What was going on? I was sure the village of Pakali was on the main river. Where were this man and the boy taking me? Could I trust them? Were they really from Pakali? I glanced nonchalantly back at the driver and he flashed me an inscrutable smile, which did nothing to alleviate my increasing concern.

It was dawning on me that I was completely at the mercy of these tribal people. If I were to mysteriously disappear, if some unfortunate incident were to occur, such as me accidentally falling into a large boiling cauldron of soup, no one would be the wiser, although some nefarious tribal people might be the fuller.

As the dugout canoe continued taking me further away from the safety of the main river, the full scope of my vulnerability was becoming clear. What had I gotten myself into? How could I not have seen through the studied casualness of the driver and the menacing child? Obviously they were up to no good.

Before I could begin formulating intricate escape plans, however, we rounded a bend and the broad Balawa River once again stretched out before us, comfortingly lacking any other islands that might confuse and confound the nervous missionary.

Chapter 4

The Day the Freak Show Came to Town

The intense scrutiny begins

Horseflies buzzed and bit mercilessly, and from time to time I had to wrench my head to the side to avoid head-on collisions with lumbering bumblebees obliviously bumbling their way along their invisible bumblebee highway, down which we were apparently going the wrong way.

The dugout shook slightly as we passed over a stretch of churning, turbulent water. Several large black boulders jutted threateningly out of the river, and small whirlpools sucked in twigs and river foam.

We rounded a bend, and a large sandbar stretched out several hundred yards along the bank. Women could be seen in the shallow water beating their clothes against a rock while nearby, naked children entertained themselves by playing and splashing and chasing each other across the sand. When they noticed us, some rushed up the riverbank and down the trail to trumpet our arrival; others made their way excitedly toward us.

There was a small waterway between the riverbank and the sandbar, and we navigated into it. The driver shut off the motor and in silence we paddled the boat toward the gathering crowd.

I was acutely aware that there was no deflecting the full force of the many eyes studying me. I looked up at the people gazing down on me and gave a hesitant wave of the hand. A very few of the onlookers returned the gesture with equal uncertainty, but most of them merely giggled nervously. Some of the children hid fearfully behind the adults. Note to self: Investigate whether or not waving is considered to be an obscene or aggressive gesture in the Wilo culture.

We ran the boat up onto the shore. It seemed as though we sat there motionless for several minutes, although in reality only a couple of seconds had ticked by when a swarm of people descended down the bank toward us. A few of them greeted me as they approached, but most of them walked right past, nimbly stepping around me while balancing on the sideboards of the canoe like circus performers walking a tightrope. They were intent on something behind me. When I turned around to see what the attraction was, I saw that all my gear was getting swooped up by the mass of people and was being carried up the bank and toward the village.

I joined the line of people, not sure where we were heading. The driver of the dugout accompanied me closely, a bit like a bodyguard protectively shadowing his charge. I was ushered into a building at the edge of the village, a building that was already full of excited people. Behind me more squeezed in. No one wanted to miss a single scene of the unfolding drama.

From all appearances, the building was used as a place for the villagers to store things, as opposed to a residence, which only confirmed the maxim that appearances can be deceiving. Over the course of the next several nights, I was to be robbed, grievously assaulted, and in many other ways subjected to much cruel and unusual treatment by the residents of this particular structure. The long-term psychological fallout of this abuse would be manifested in me primarily as a loathing of all things rodent.

For now, those residents were making themselves scarce. The Wilos were pressed up tight against each other, but the driver made sure there was a small bubble of space around me. Everyone was jockeying for position and looking at me with open, unabashed curiosity. The windows and doorway were filled with faces peering in. I didn't know which was worse: the weight of the many eyes on me, or the unnatural silence that settled on everybody as they waited to see what I would do or say.

Eventually a few of the Wilo men stepped forward and tried

out their Spanish on me, but after the greetings and a few basic questions and answers had been spoken, their Spanish was exhausted. Another long and uncomfortable silence ensued, broken only when someone noticed the soccer ball I had brought. I was practically blinded by the many faces in the room that lit up with pleasure when I unpacked the ball. The Wilos were beginning to adopt soccer as a form of community entertainment, and the soccer ball was a big hit. And I, by association, was a hit as well.

This building was to be my temporary residence while the finishing touches were placed on my mud-and-thatch house. I went to sleep that night wondering what the morning would bring. I planned to get up early, go out to the proposed airstrip site, and start leveling ground, felling trees, and filling holes. I was hoping a few of the Wilos would give me a hand with the work, but there were no guarantees. Nothing had been mentioned about them helping.

Chapter 5

Airstrip Angst 101

Build an airstrip in the jungle? No sweat!

The morning sun had yet to crest the hill behind the village when I was awakened by what sounded like the clanging of a bell. Swinging my feet out of the hammock, I would have walked over to the door to look out, but realized there was no need. The walls of my temporary residence reached only half-way up to the roof. Standing, as I was, in the middle of the room, I had a 360-degree view of everything outside.

This also meant that I could be viewed from any of 360 degrees, a fact the neighborhood children had already figured out and were taking full advantage of, judging from the many inquisitive eyes peeking over the wall at me.

I looked beyond the eyes and saw a trail of Wilos streaming through the village, led by an elderly man who was striking a machete against a beat-up old shovel as he walked purposefully along. Those following behind him were similarly equipped for work. My heart sank at the sight. Perhaps yesterday I should have expressly asked that a few of the men stay behind to help me with the work of clearing the airstrip site. Even though I hadn't fully expected the Wilos to put the work of their day-to-day survival on hold in order to help me make the airstrip, I had been harboring a small degree of hope that a few would choose to help, at least initially. But from what I was seeing, practically the entire village was leaving, heading out to who knows where.

Oh well. I had a lot of work ahead, and I might as well get started. I quickly got a few tools together and made my way through the village and out toward the site where the airstrip was to be built.

Along the way I passed several people, and was relieved to see that the intense, incessant scrutiny I had been subjected to the previous day was gone. In its place was a mild timidity mingled, at least in the case of the children, with a desire to play with danger. A young boy stepped away from his small group of friends, facial features set in an expression of defiant bravado. He took several calculated paces toward me and then ran away, laughing in giddy exhilaration.

A few of the adults spoke to me with sounds that meant nothing to me, but their expressions were friendly and open, and I returned their smiles, greeting them in Spanish, although doubting they would understand. In my wake were formed small groups of people murmuring *sotto voce*, as they discussed their evaluation of this brief encounter with the white foreigner who couldn't speak right.

There was little I could do about the condition of my pigmentation, but I did have on my person a couple of tools that would help me begin to remedy the part about not being able to speak right. I opened up a small notebook and began scribbling down what I heard the people around me saying. I could only catch bits and pieces of what was being said, and I couldn't understand what any of it meant, but I jotted it down anyway, as best I could. Let the learning begin. The fact that learning often begins with failure and embarrassment didn't escape my mind.

I made my way past the perimeter houses of the village, through a little wooded area where my house was being built, and walked across the village soccer pitch. I arrived at the airstrip site and discovered that the early morning sun was already beating down with a dismaying intensity. Under its bright glare several dozen Wilo people were working. Some were swinging machetes; others were piling grass and leaves onto woven mats and hauling them off to the side. A group of men was gathered around a large tree, apparently discussing the best way to fell it and remove it from the airstrip site.

The older man who had led the procession through the village had staked out a small knoll and was shoveling and scraping and smoothing it down to a level plane. Clad in a pair of ragged blue overalls, and possessed of a quick and infectious laugh, Disu was someone with whom I felt instantly at ease. The dugout driver of yesterday was nearby, and I was to later learn that his name was Odowiya.

When I approached, most of them stopped and looked at me, their gaze taking in the pick, shovel, and rake I held in my hands. Surprise registered on their faces, and comments were made. Had they perhaps expected my participation to be limited to sitting under the shade of a tree and shouting out an occasional directive or observation between sips of cool coconut juice?

I smiled at no one in particular, walked over and began shoveling opposite Disu, who along with Odowiya, seemed the least fazed by my presence. I was already sweating, so I might as well start working. I just wished I had some kind of clue as to how to go about building this airstrip. And I had overlooked bringing work gloves with me. This was not an auspicious beginning.

Chapter 6

A Gift (I Think) from Kanem

Don't show the new guy anything you're not willing to part with!

"Dah-wee, where are you coming from?" Kanem asks me.

"From the river," I answer. So far so good.

"Oh, were you getting a bath?" she asks with great interest.

"Yes, I was," I reply somewhat nervously. At this point I'm cringing a bit because I'm sure that, like most of my conversations with the Wilos, this one is soon to spiral out of control, beyond my ability to understand, or to correct any possible misunderstandings, much less to attempt an intelligible reply. Maybe she would just say "*Ha-oh*" and we could both go about our business thinking I speak her language pretty well. That'd be nice, for a change.

My hopeful thoughts, though, are both interrupted and dashed as she puts down the broom she is sweeping her yard with, and poses this question to me: "Gibberish, gibberish, gibberish?"

I smile and give her an apologetic shrug. She chuckles and murmurs something to herself. She turns her back to me, but only for an instant. When she turns back around, she is holding something in her hand, something that is frantically flailing to escape her clutches.

Kanem motions me over and I see that the creature in her hand happens to be a large crab. I can't be sure, but I think she's holding it out for me to take, so I gingerly accept it and say, "OK, good."

She laughs again and, mission accomplished, returns to her work of keeping the dirt around her house free of weeds and litter.

I continue on to my own house, still unsure if she had wanted me to take the crab, or just look at it.

Oh well, I would just have to get used to being unsure about what everyone around me was saying, and what their actions implied. For their part, Kanem and the other Wilos would have to get used to not showing me things they weren't willing to part with.

Kanem was such a nice person. She was an elderly widow. Her husband, like almost all his Wilo contemporaries, had grown up deep in the jungle, living in isolation and dreading the powerful witchcraft of neighboring tribes. The far-away drone of an outboard motor, or the hum of an approaching airplane would send him and his family scurrying to hide themselves, lest their presence become known.

His wasn't the idyllic and innocent upbringing that many might imagine. Fear of the evil spirits consumed his people, and life had to be lived in such a way that those spirits would not interfere with their pursuit of a happy and successful life. Despair was a constant companion as he and his people saw the disparity between their own spiritual powers and the more impressive powers of other tribes. When he and others would gather sufficient courage to tentatively interact with neighboring tribes, they would often find themselves the brunt of ridicule and contempt because of their backward ways.

Kanem's husband grew up to become very influential among the Wilos. He was one of the main advocates of getting missionaries to come live among them and teach the Word of God to his people. He died without seeing his wishes come to fruition. As far as we know, he died without once having had an opportunity to really understand God's good news.

Kanem and the other Wilos now lived in villages, unlike the Wilos of generations past who had lived scattered throughout the jungle in small family groups. Many of the Wilos now wore clothing, cooked using aluminum pots, struck matches to start their fires, and used line and hook to catch their fish. But many of the old fears persisted.

Kanem was getting quite old. So were several others in the village. Did we missionaries arrive too late to give these senior citizens the chance to hear and understand God's Word? For Kanem's husband it certainly was too late. We often prayed for Kanem and others like her in the village, that they would remain healthy during our time of language and culture study. Maybe it wouldn't be too late for them.

Chapter 7

The Love Affair

Love is in the air when I engage the communications radio

While some of us focused on working at the airstrip site, a few men went about putting the finishing touches on what was to be my house. The walls, which consisted of dozens of poles placed vertically several inches apart, with mud filling in the spaces between, were completed. The thatch on the roof had been layered and tied down tightly with jungle vines to the web of poles that served as rafters and trusses. The Wilos, though, were not quite finished. They wanted to plaster a thin layer of mud over the walls to cover the poles and fill in the cracks, making the house a little more bug proof. I was not inclined to object.

I was, however, greatly anticipating the day I could move into my own place. I had spent the past ten days living in the fishbowl that was the community storage shed. The complete lack of privacy in there was wearing, and I was also getting tired of all the harassment I was being subjected to by the resident rats. It was time I had my own place.

It was also, I determined, about time for me to attempt to communicate with people on the outside. Nobody had heard from me since the airplane had dropped me off at the airstrip downriver in Poleni, over a week ago. I was sure that, if there happened to be some people out there who hadn't immediately forgotten me once I headed into the jungle, they would likely be wondering what was happening with me. For all they knew, I might still be stuck in Poleni, waiting at the river with my thumb out.

So one evening I dug out the communications radio and the

antenna. I lugged it all over to where my house was being built. Several people followed me, and as word of this new development spread throughout the village, swarms of people began buzzing about, crowding around, shouting out orders and questions and myriad other grammatical constructions to one another, none of which I understood.

Most of the Wilos were familiar with radios, and they knew how antennas were set up. Soon a guy named Lama, a lanky fellow with a surprisingly bright smile in spite of the conspicuous absence of several teeth, took the antenna from me. He carried it over to a straight but short tree and began climbing.

Wait! Not that tree! Lama had chosen to climb a young tree that was little more than a sapling. We wouldn't get much reception if the antenna were placed in such a short tree. I had been planning on stringing it from the tall cashew tree.

I debated whether to stop Lama and try to explain why the antenna should go on the taller tree. But he had already climbed into the upper branches of the sapling, so I decided to just go with the flow. That's when I noticed that the tree Lama was climbing was beginning to bend under his weight. Not at all concerned, he continued climbing higher until the branch he was on bumped up against the cashew tree. He quickly transferred to the taller tree and continued climbing. He fastened the antenna high in the tree and then slid back down to the ground, reminiscent of a fireman descending the fire station pole.

We ran the two ends of the antenna to a couple of other trees, hooked up the radio to the antenna and the battery, and then we waited impatiently for seven o'clock to arrive. That was the time when the missionaries customarily turned on their sets so they could share the news from their various jungle locations.

Seven o'clock found a dozen of us huddled around the radio as I hit the power button and tuned in to the proper frequency. We were immediately listening in on a conversation.

The policy was that all communication on the radio be carried out in Spanish so as not to offend those of our host country who might be listening in. Some of the Wilos standing around me strained to listen to the disembodied voices coming from the radio in the hopes of catching a familiar word or two. I simply sat there on the dirt floor soaking up the conversation of my far-away coworkers. I suddenly didn't feel quite so alone.

When the two missionaries concluded their conversation, I picked up the mic and thought about what I would say. I already knew who I would call. Don was an administrator for our organization, and he had been instrumental in getting the ministry among the Wilo people off the ground. He also happened to be the radio operator in town. On the radio, Don used words sparingly, much like a telegram sender keeps the message short and succinct in order to economize. So I formulated what I would say accordingly.

I cleared my voice, keyed the mic, and spoke the call numbers for Don. There was a pause, then his voice responded, "Go ahead, Davey. I'm copying you." He sounded bored, but nevertheless with those words, Don took up a special place in my heart.

I didn't expect him to say much more though, so I encapsulated the past ten days simply by saying that I had arrived at Pakali and everything was fine.

"Roger," Don enthused.

"OK, there's no other traffic from this end. Greetings! Pakali signing off," I said, expecting that to be the end of the conversation.

"Well, how is everything going in there?" Don continued, surprising me into momentary silence. When did Don become so verbose? I told him that the work on the airstrip was progressing quickly, and that all was well.

"OK, Davey. We're praying for you out here," Don replied.

This simple radio conversation marked the beginning of a meaningful relationship in my life, a relationship that would help me through the early years of isolation and loneliness in the jungle. It was the kind of relationship many men of our Western society can relate to – namely, that between a man and an electronic device. I fell in love with the radio. From that day on, the radio schedule became a daily part of my life. My workday would start every morning at 6:15 when I would turn on the radio to answer roll call and to give weather reports to the missionary pilots who might be flying through our area on that particular day. Every evening at 7:00 I would again turn on the radio to participate in the evening radio schedule.

Throughout the following years, it was to be the radio that would bring us news of things such as tribal people responding to the message of the gospel. It was to be the radio that would inform us of co-workers' sicknesses, or of their struggles to contain rampant sickness among the tribal people they worked with. It was over the radio that we would learn of family or friends giving birth, or of deaths in the family. And on more than one occasion our small missionary team was to sit huddled around the radio practically all day long, prayerfully listening to search-and-rescue operations being conducted for an airplane that had gone missing.

The radio would be our primary link to the outside world. One day it would even provide a primitive yet very welcome avenue through which we could send and receive email. But that day was still several years down the road.

Chapter 8

The Tree of Encouragement

God can send encouragement even through a dead tree

At first I couldn't see the tree for the forest surrounding it. It wasn't until I had been in Pakali for two weeks that my eyes finally focused in on it, and I saw it for what it was. It stood as a sentinel in a grouping of trees that grew between the new airstrip site and the river.

One evening, as was my wont, I had taken a stroll out to the clearing that was looking more and more like an airstrip every day. I carried with me a sturdy stick sharpened on one end. With every step, I jabbed the stick into the ground to test the integrity of the surface. More often than not the first surface to give way was the skin on my hands; but sometimes I would hear or sense a hollowness in the ground, and upon digging down a bit, the earth would open up to expose a big hole. Pilots, I had been told, don't like that sort of thing. These holes were usually caused by rotted tree roots or by dastard colonies of ants with whom we were to carry out a long and protracted battle for dominance of the airstrip.

To make sure no dangerous hollows were lurking beneath the surface waiting to open up at the touch of an airplane wheel, practically every inch of the airstrip surface had to be tested. That's what I did during my daily evening walks.

So it was that she finally caught my eye. I had just finished shoveling dirt into a hole and as I straightened up I glanced off to the right and there she was, clear as day. The setting sun brought the tree into sharp relief and I found myself looking at God's encouragement to me… a stick figure of the Statue of Liberty!

Before I was even born God had caused that tree to sprout. He had caused a seedling to take root and grow up tall and sturdy along the banks of the Balawa River. During the years that I was growing up, playing with Lego, fishing and swimming, attending school, and playing sports, this tree was surviving floods and dry spells, fires and tropical storms. It eventually grew to be taller than any of the other surrounding trees, breaking through the jungle canopy and reaching to the sky.

The Amazon jungle being the harsh environment that it is, something eventually had gotten to the tree. It lost its leaves, its roots stopped sending sufficient life to the trunk, and it was reduced to a tall, dead sentinel looking down on the greenery beneath it. The bare branches reached out from the trunk in such a way that it resembled, at least to my weary mind, the Statue of Liberty.

It had been a long day. I smiled and shook my head wryly. I looked away and continued working. A few minutes later, though, I looked up again and she was still standing there.

From that day on, my eyes were often drawn to that tree, and a warm if somewhat ironic sense of comfort would wash over me. It was odd: a Canadian, living in the Amazon jungle, was finding encouragement in a tree that vaguely resembled an iconic statue given to the United States by France many years ago.

When I was finally able to move into my permanent home, that Statue of Liberty was clearly visible from my little kitchen table. In the early mornings I would sit with a hot cup of coffee cradled in my hands and lose my gaze in the tree as I would remember friends and family and a life far away from the jungle.

After several years this Pakali Statue of Liberty eventually succumbed to the wear and tear of being dead, which can be considerable. She toppled over, disappearing from view, and was later unceremoniously used as firewood. By that time, though, I was prepared for life without her.

Chapter 9

Jungle Junk Food

The Wilo people get the munchies

One hot, muggy afternoon (were there any other kinds of afternoon in the jungle?) I heard a commotion. It sounded like some pots banging together, and the animated voices of people passing by, outside my window.

I was not disappointed to have an excuse to get up and stretch. I put down the notebook of Wilo words and phrases I had been studiously perusing, and went to the kitchen window to see what was happening. It looked like a community outing of some sort. Moms, dads, grandmas, grandpas, children and dogs were all boisterously making their way past my house and across the soccer pitch. They were heading out, they informed me, to get some jungle treats, kind of like their equivalent of junk food. They were hungry for some snacks. OK, I'll say it – they all had the munchies.

Out past the end of the soccer pitch the foragers found what they were looking for. Now the real fun began. With machetes, knives, and other assorted sharp instruments they started digging, and soon were plucking things up and depositing them into their containers. From a distance it looked as though they were picking strawberries.

Occasionally a shout of pain would reach my ears. I would look out the window and see someone hopping around a bit. Others nearby would mask their sympathy and concern with much merry laughter as they observed the misfortune of the shouter. All would continue filling their small aluminum pots.

An hour or so later the entire group came traipsing back, the people with full containers and the dogs with silly grins on their faces, possibly amused by the antics of their humans. A few of the guys stopped to show me their junk food.

In the container was what looked like ant soup. No, it looked more like a pool party for ants. A bunch of red, inch-long ants were floating in two inches of water. Some were doing the backstroke, others the breaststroke. A few were attempting to scale the sides of the container, while others entertained themselves with a game that required them to walk from one side of the container to the other without getting wet. It looked like they were having fun.

"Well," I thought with a twinge of satisfaction, "*these* are some ants that won't be burrowing holes under the airstrip anymore."

The lid closed, but I imagine the pool party continued, at least for a while, until the partiers were roasted over an open fire. I was informed that the proper etiquette was to eat the ants along with cassava bread. But with these particular ants you do not eat the head, of course. That would be gross and disgusting and most likely would clog the arteries. I wondered vaguely if they might taste any better with salt and vinegar but figured I could find out some other time.

A few of the Wilos had blood trickling down their feet, which was what all the hopping around and laughing had been about. More often than not the Wilos walked around barefoot, no worse for the wear, since their feet developed protective calluses. But these red ants were well endowed with big craniums fitted with large pinchers. And apparently some of them had been determined to get in the first bite.

Later that night a few of the villagers came by to visit. In their hands they carried several of these ants. They assured me that if I were to eat some of them, it would help me learn to speak the Wilo language more quickly.

"Really?" I asked weakly. I looked down at the ants, and they looked back. Well, not much else was working. It was worth a shot.

Chapter 10

Best Show in Town

The Tru (White) Man Show

Finally the day came when I was given the keys to my new home. OK, so there were no keys. There were no keys for the simple reason that there was no lock on the door. There was no lock on the door because – you guessed it – there was no door.

Fortunately, there *was* a doorway. Stepping through it and into my house was actually a bit like stepping into a cave. The thatched roof kept the house quite cool, and the absence of windows caused it to be very, very dark inside. Apparently I was not the only one to think it was like a cave inside the house; a couple of bats had already staked out prime hanging space in the leaves of the roof. There were no partitions; it was one big cavernous room.

I chose a corner of the house to be my bedroom, and swung my hammock from two big rafters that spanned the width of my new residence. There would be no hiding from the gaze of curious people who might peek through the doorway; privacy would have to be postponed for now.

There was no plumbing. There was no electric wiring. There were no cabinets, no closets. It was four mud-and-pole walls, two open doorways through which all the village animals came and went freely, a dirt floor with roots breaking through the surface here and there, and palm thatch topping it all off. After my nights in the storage shed, my house was truly a thing a beauty.

A large group of Wilos had streamed into the house with me. They stood around watching as I strung my hammock and organized my things. I tried to formulate some small talk, but as usual, one or two minutes of light conversation pretty much exhausted both my mind and my repertoire of the Wilo language. After a few moments of silence that no one seemed to find uncomfortable except me, I sat down in my hammock, got out a book, and in vain tried to read in the dim light streaming through the doorway.

I was apparently the best show in town, and watching me read kept the Wilos entertained for another ten or fifteen minutes. But observing inertia in action can be tedious even for the entertainment deprived, and the Wilos eventually decided to find excitement elsewhere.

"OK, Dah-wee, we're going home now," they said cheerfully.

"OK, go home," I replied with equal cheer. Would I ever get used to saying that? It sounded terribly rude to my proper Canadian ears, but that was the polite way of saying goodbye in the Wilo language.

They left, and I continued reading, but not without pausing momentarily to reflect on how I was like a TV set for these tribal people, a window through which they could gaze upon a limitless amount of curious and foreign scenes. No doubt they would be ecstatic when my co-workers arrived, as that would provide them the option of changing channels.

It wasn't long before more visitors entered the doorway. These ones glanced at me but said nothing. After determining that I posed little danger, they began poking about, wandering throughout the house. I initially tried to ignore them, hoping they would soon move along of their own accord, but it was not to be.

Eventually I had my fill of being distracted by their presence. I didn't want them to assume they had free access to this house. I picked up a stick and started toward them.

They seemed startled at first by my sinister approach, then indignant. Finally, resigned to the inevitable, they allowed me to herd them through the doorway. The last thing I needed was a bunch of chickens and roosters snooping around inside my house, nesting in the rafters and depositing their calling cards randomly about on my nice new dirt floor.

Chapter 11

The Art of Conversing

Taking baby steps down the trail of language learning

On another front, my oratory skills in the Wilo language were showing definite signs of improvement. By way of illustration, one day, as was becoming a regular custom, I took a meandering walk through town – town being the cluster of several dozen houses that comprised the center of the village of Pakali.

I saw a man seated on a piece of wood in front of his house, so I ambled over and sat down beside him. He asked me a few things in his language that I didn't understand and I answered with a few things in his language that he didn't understand either. It was comforting to see that I was not the only one who struggled with this language.

I happened to notice a mangy dog trying to doze off in the shade of a nearby mango tree. Seeing a chance to display my new-found prowess in Wilo communication, I pointed to the dog and said, "That's a dog." The man sitting beside me followed my gaze and nodded.

Further demonstrating my speaking ability, I expounded, "That's not a cat." The man agreed.

I was warming to my subject by that time and went on to explain effusively that it wasn't a parrot either. The man nodded yet again, his noncommittal expression successfully masking his awe of my language learning ability, not to mention my enviable understanding of the various species. Alas, this conversation of ours came to an abrupt halt when the topic of our discussion lazily opened an eye, saw our unusual interest in him, and slunk away, glancing nervously over his shoulder at me.

Any designs I might have had on preserving an austere, sophisticated image were thrown out the window long ago. I tried out my newly learned phrases on any listening ear, be it human, canine, feline or fowl. Even the face in the mirror didn't escape being subjected to these monotonous performances on a regular basis.

Villagers would stop by the house throughout the day to teach me more words or phrases, and it seemed like everybody had a different way of saying the exact same thing. They kept reminding me that their language was easy; after all, if the little children of the village could speak it, surely their new missionary would learn it quickly and expeditiously.

"Our language is straight," they rarely failed to assure me. To help me picture just how straight it was, they would crook their arm, palm facing downward, and draw a straight line out until their arm was fully extended, much like a one-armed baseball umpire signaling a base runner to be safe at home.

The Wilos liked nothing better than to come by and have me say all that I could in their language. Teaching me their language had become something of a community project. They would quiz me on all the different kinds of trees in the jungle, or the many kinds of fish in the river. They had never witnessed someone making a concerted attempt to learn their language, and they were quite convinced that if I could learn long lists of vocabulary, I would then be a fluent speaker.

What about grammar? What about syntax? Well, none of the Wilos had thought much about such things. Their language didn't even have a word for "word". Certainly their language did have a grammatical structure to it; it's just that no one among them had ever analyzed it. At this point, theirs was exclusively a spoken language. It had no written form. The Wilos had never seen a single sentence of their language written down on paper. Their understanding of the inner workings of their language was extremely limited, even though they spoke it perfectly.

So, I would try to learn their long lists of vocabulary, and at the same time would keep my ears open in the hopes of capturing a phrase now and then, something with some grammatical meat to it.

In the early months this was no easy feat. Just writing down a simple phrase was quite an adventure, for both me and the poor soul who happened to utter it. I could only manage to catch a few sounds at a time, so I would have to ask them to repeat the phrase again. And again. And again. Quite often they would repeat it differently each time. Then I would attempt to repeat it back to them to their satisfaction. I would try to determine what it meant. And finally I would attempt to ascertain how many words the phrase contained. At times, even when successful, these linguistical endeavors ended in discouragement, such as when, after much concentration and labor, I discovered that the phrase *bitemaokwododiweneinawahwibo* was actually five words that translated roughly as "This-guy our language still is-an-ignorant one." Yeah, I get that a lot.

There was very little that was easy for me at this stage of the game. Even just listening to the Wilos talk to each other was exhausting. The one thing that was encouraging was the enthusiasm of the Wilo people. None of them seemed inclined to give up on me, so I continued plodding ahead.

I tried valiantly and vainly to remember the names of all the trees. I would go fishing with the Wilos and rack my brain for the correct name of some obscure fish that one of them just caught. And although at times I felt like a show dog jumping through hoops and being raced around an obstacle course, I was always thankful for the eagerness and excitement of the Wilos in teaching me. They made this tedious and, at times, torturous process enjoyable and fun... most of the time.

Chapter 12

The First Landing

The new airstrip is tested by a bush pilot

After a few weeks of working on the airstrip, it was decided that a pilot would land to evaluate the strip and to give guidance on further work that needed to be done. The drone of the approaching airplane was a wonderful sound indeed. It swooped low over the airstrip once, then again, and finally it circled around for the final approach. It dropped out of view behind a small knoll, and the next thing we saw was the airplane taxiing down the strip toward us.

Actually, "taxiing" may not be the operative word to describe what it was doing. It sounded more like it was engaged in a desperate tug-of-war with a sinister but invisible force pulling against it. The engine was screaming as the plane struggled to make its way down the dirt strip toward our group of apprehensive onlookers. As it drew near, I could see that in spite of our best attempts at packing down the surface dirt, the wheels of the airplane were still sinking deep into the soft ground. It didn't look or sound like a safe and friendly landing experience for the pilot.

When he finally arrived at our end of the strip, the pilot swung the tail around so the plane was pointing back down the runway. I wasn't exactly sure what frame of mind he might be in at this point. Would he be satisfied and relieved with simply being alive after such a harrowing landing, or would he insist on premature death or at least some kind of partial dismemberment for all involved in the runway construction?

The door swung open, and Ronald stepped out of the airplane. "How are things going in here?" he asked calmly, proffering his hand. I stepped forward and shook it, but only after surreptitiously checking that it contained no sharp instruments.

"You tell me," I replied, and the sound of English coming from my lips was unexpectedly comforting. "Seemed like the plane was struggling just to taxi down the runway."

"Oh, that. No, I was just doing a few things to test the surface of the dirt." Ronald flashed a friendly smile at the crowd of excited spectators. His expression said that this was just another day at the office. Who doesn't risk life and limb undertaking the first landing on a jungle airstrip made by a green missionary and tribal people who had rarely even seen an airplane up close? No big deal.

And not only did this pilot possess what appeared to be nerves of steel, but he also possessed, perhaps as a result of the power of repetitive reinforcement, an understanding of the priorities of people such as me; he reached into the plane and pulled out a mailbag.

So, what did he think of the airstrip? Well, other than the small detail that there were still too many trees obstructing the approach, and the fact that the ground was still dangerously soft, and that the strip was too narrow, everything seemed pretty good. Oh yeah, and about that gently sloping gully traversing the middle of the strip – the one that had almost caused the plane to launch back into the air – it would definitely have to be filled in.

Hmmm. My grade point average in airstrip making appeared to be rather low. I could live with that, but the next people to land perhaps wouldn't. We still had plenty of work to do.

Nevertheless, I considered this first landing to be a smashing success, in that no smashing whatsoever occurred. I determined not to encourage Ronald with this positive perspective, though, and instead took note of the things he suggested we do to improve the airstrip.

While Ronald and I talked, most of the Wilo people gathered around the airplane. Some of them had never seen an airplane other than those that would fly overhead occasionally. They took advantage of this opportunity to get an up-close look. They carefully inspected it from tail to propeller, as though they were intending to build one themselves sometime soon. They animatedly carried on a running commentary as each part fell under their scrutiny.

When Ronald was ready to leave, he motioned for everybody to stand away from the airplane. He climbed in, started the engine, and the plane began slowly lumbering down the airstrip. At the far end, he turned the plane around toward us, gunned the engine, and the plane began picking up speed, although not enough for my liking. It rolled down the shallow gully and up again, earthbound still. Finally, as the plane roared past us, the soft ground relaxed its grip and released the plane into the sky.

A month later, I was joined by my co-worker Tim. We would spend the next couple of months doing some more work on the airstrip, and fixing up our houses before Tim's wife and daughter and the rest of our missionary team arrived.

So it was that by the end of 1992, our team of one family and four singles was settling into the routines of jungle life and ministry. Tim and Laurie, with baby Ashley, were my new neighbors and were living in their brand-new rustic house. Much like mine, their house was built by the tribal people and had few amenities. Our houses were little more than four mud walls and a palm-leaf roof, and they would remain rustic during the initial years that we dedicated to learning the language and culture of the Wilos.

Phyllis and Elvia had arrived together and lived for a while in a tiny, run-down, decrepit hut in the heart of the village. Of all our missionary team, they experienced the worst living conditions during these early days, but they took it in their stride. The place that they initially called home was overrun by rats, and provided barely enough room to swing two hammocks. It was so bad that when we eventually were able to obtain and set up a tent for them, it was a great improvement.

Betilde rounded out our team. She and Elvia were national missionaries sent out by their respective churches, and we were excited to have a team that included them.

We didn't fully appreciate it at the time, but God had brought together a missionary team that would work well as a unit. We would spend years in a stressful environment working toward a single objective, living in very close proximity to one another. We had differing views and opinions, a wide range of likes and dislikes, individual convictions, idiosyncrasies, and personalities. To top it all off, Elvia and Betilde spoke no English, so we had to contend not only with the language and cultural barriers of Wilo society, but with language and cultural barriers on our own team as well.

We rolled up our sleeves and went to work learning to communicate in this strange Wilo language. We knew we had our work cut out for us, but mercifully none of us suspected just how many years would have to be dedicated to this first step of ministry.

Chapter 13

No Alligators Allowed

Surely spearing fish among the alligators can't be a good idea

Yanako came by my house early one morning. He was a robust man, built along the lines of a sumo wrestler. He was the captain of the village, and a more unassuming captain there could never be. Wilo society wasn't built around a strong leadership structure, perhaps a result of the earlier generations of Wilos living scattered throughout the jungle, as opposed to living together in villages. Each individual Wilo family went about doing their own thing in their own time at their own pace, and there was really not much influence that Yanako had, or wanted to have over that.

But his leadership was not inconsequential by any means. He was an important village spokesman, a liaison of sorts with the national government, and a determined defender of village well-being.

He was also incredibly difficult to understand. When he spoke Wilo, the sounds would burst from his mouth like water from a fireman's hose, practically bowling me over, extinguishing any flicker of hope I might have had of understanding him. When he chose to speak in Spanish, he did so with equal enthusiasm but with atrocious grammar and perplexing vocabulary.

He and his wife were frequent visitors to my house, often stopping by on their way back from their garden to ask if I wanted to buy a stalk of bananas they had brought back, or perhaps trade something for it. I assumed that's why he was at my door bright and early that morning.

"Hi, Yanako. Did you awaken well?" I was starting to get the hang of this language.

"Yes, Dah-wee, I awoke well. Hey, I've come to ask you something. Do you want to go spearing fish today?"

"Yes, I want some bananas," I promptly responded.

"What?" I could tell from his confused expression that my answer had taken him by surprise. That was never a good sign.

"Umm, what did you ask at first?" I asked.

"Do you want to go with us to spear fish over at the lagoon?"

"Oh. Sure," I replied nonchalantly, hoping he hadn't noticed that I had just said something completely ridiculous. When Yanako talked, my only hope at understanding him was to catch a word or two and then fill in the blanks as best I could. In this instance the first two syllables out of his mouth had made up the word for "bananas", so I had just gone with that.

I didn't want to have to try and explain all this to him, and was relieved when he didn't follow up on my gaffe.

"Good. Let's go," was all he said.

"Right now?" I asked him, while my stomach growled, *what about my breakfast?*

"Yes, we're leaving right now," he replied.

He waited for me while I jumped into my bathing suit. As we were walking down to the river he said, "I'll bring you some bananas tomorrow."

About a dozen guys were waiting for us in the canoe when we got there. They must have all been ready to head out when someone had said, "Here's a crazy idea: let's see if the missionary wants to come along with us."

I needn't have worried about breakfast either, as it turned out. It was served onboard. While we slowly paddled across the wide river, smoked fish and cassava cakes were passed around. Yanako made sure I got my share; apparently he was to be my host on this excursion.

Reaching the far side of the river, we came to the entrance of a small waterway that had been invisible until we got to within a few feet of it. We nosed the canoe into the stream and began making our way up it. It was like entering into a mythical world. The surface of the water was a smooth pane of smoked glass. Only the hardiest beams of sunlight were able to fight their way through the blanket of branches under which our canoe silently glided. The normal tangle of underbrush was noticeably absent, and the piercing calls of birds filled out the impression that I was passing through a jungle sanctuary.

A few minutes later we broke out into a long lagoon that was the size of several football fields strung together end to end. As we paddled the length of the lagoon, sinister pairs of eyes surfaced with barely a ripple, following our progress for a while, and just as silently disappearing again.

Not good. Those eyes had probably never seen white meat before. Nobody had said we'd have to fight off alligators with one hand while spearing fish with the other.

At the far end, a small stream was feeding into the lagoon. We made our way a short distance up it and then the Wilos started jumping out of the canoe. The water was shallow; only waist deep. This was where the fish spearing was to take place.

In many ways the Wilos were a culture in transition. They continued living a life similar to generations gone by; they occupied themselves with much the same things their ancestors had done before them. What made this generation different was that they had access to tools and equipment that their ancestors had never dreamed of having.

I wasn't too surprised, then, to see that most of the Wilos were donning goggles. In no time at all everybody was absorbed in spearing fish. Walking about in the shallow waters, they were all bent over at the waist, with their heads and shoulders submerged as they searched out the hiding-places of the fish.

I was slow to follow suit. I hadn't seen a "NO ALLIGATORS ALLOWED" sign posted anywhere, so I wasn't sure what was to prevent those hungry alligator eyes from surfacing right beside me. I decided my best course of action would be to stay close to Yanako. He had invited me, so of all the fish spearers he'd probably feel the worst about one of these curious gators taking a bite out of me, with the notable exception of myself, needless to say.

That's what I would do; I would get in the water and stick close to Yanako. That being decided, I was about to jump out of the canoe when I realized I didn't know which one he was. As I scanned the surface, all I could see was an array of butts bobbing in the water. At that moment I was very thankful that the Wilos wear shorts while spearing fish.

The people inside the shorts were surfacing only long enough to catch another breath before going back under, not giving me a chance to identify Yanako among the goggled faces. To my relief, I eventually caught a glimpse of what looked like a sumo wrestler. That would be him. With my host in view, or at least that part of him, I eased into the cold water and made my way in that direction. If any alligators were going to get me, they'd have to go through him first, and if it came to that, I wouldn't be betting against Yanako.

Chapter 14

Not Knowing if You're Coming or Going

If I'm returning home, don't ask me where I'm going

Tim and I were out behind his house, looking into a deep hole that had been dug in the process of making his mud-and-thatch residence. At some point, we were hoping to lay down some plastic piping from the spring that was located at the base of a nearby hill, and run it down to the village. The Wilos were excited about the prospect of not having to go so far to get their drinking water, and we were hoping we could pipe running water into our houses as well. With that in mind, we were discussing the possibility of making a lid to cover this hole so it could be used as a septic tank.

In the distance we saw Buchi exiting his house. Since the first day we had arrived, Buchi had been one of our most frequent visitors. He had taken us under his wing, always checking in on us and making sure we were doing OK.

He was heading out toward the airstrip, but when he noticed us he made a detour in our direction, curious to see what we were doing. He knew how to speak Spanish in a broken but understandable manner, and up to this point most of our conversations with him had been conducted in Spanish. So it caught him by surprise when Tim tried out a newly learned Wilo phrase on him.

"Where are you going?" Tim asked.

"What?"

"Where are you going?" Tim repeated, a look of uncertainty crossing his face as he began to wonder if he was pronouncing it correctly.

However, with this second attempt, a broad smile broke out across Buchi's face. "I'm going over there," he replied in his language, gesturing with his chin toward the direction he was heading. This reply was not necessarily too informative, but I think he knew that it was about as much information as we could absorb in his language at that early stage.

Tim said, "OK. Go."

"Yes, I'm going," he replied, and with a smile similar to that of a father who is proud of his son's accomplishment, he took leave and went his way.

I looked at Tim. "That went well," I said, stating the obvious.

"Little victories," Tim replied.

He was right. Little victories, mixed in among a forest of failures: that was the best way to describe our early language learning experience. Of course, I would have loved to be like Kevin Costner's character in the movie *Dances With Wolves*: someone who carefully listens to the tribal people speak and then one day simply begins talking, tentatively yet accurately.

But no, it appeared that the only way I was going to learn this language was to blunder my way to fluency. That wasn't necessarily my strategy, mind you, but all too often it was my reality. Apparently no amount of training in phonetics, phonemics, or linguistics was going to immunize me from the dreaded Blunders Disease. During those early months of language learning, I often didn't know if I was coming or going.

So, little victories were very sweet. This particular little victory of Tim's was so sweet, in fact, that the next day I determined to taste it myself. I got my chance when I noticed Buchi walking past my window toward his house. As I rushed over to the window I was rehearsing in my mind how I would say it.

"Buchi, where are you going?" I shouted through the window.

"What?" he asked.

No problem. This was just how it had gone down yesterday, I thought. He should get it the second time around.

"Where are you going?" I repeated hopefully, anticipating the big, proud smile that would crease his face again.

I was rewarded with only a puzzled look. He walked over and asked me to say it again. He really wanted to understand what I was trying to say.

I was eventually able to explain what I had meant to say, but by that time all the fun had been sucked out of the moment. When he finally realized what I was attempting to ask him, Buchi told me, "I'm not going anywhere. I'm returning home."

What? That doesn't count? Isn't going home going somewhere? Couldn't he just have answered, "I'm going home"?

And so, through failure, I had learned something else about the Wilo language. Coming and going were very specific, always spoken of in relation to the place where your travel had originated from. A Wilo never *goes* home, but rather *returns* home. Because Buchi was returning home when I asked him where he was going, he didn't even understand the question. A Wilo speaker would have asked, "Where are you returning from?"

With this, we realized how vital it was for us to know whether the Wilos were coming or going, and for that we needed to know where each of the Wilo people lived. We decided to draw up a map of the village houses and do an informal census to familiarize ourselves with who lived in which house. With the village comprising more than a hundred houses, it would be no small task. But once armed with that information, we would know when to ask the Wilos where they were going, and when to ask them where they were returning from.

Chapter 15

Jaguars, Butterflies, and Missing Persons

Village incidents reveal a society permeated by fear

Admittedly, jaguars, butterflies, and missing persons don't have a lot in common, although it is entirely possible for jaguars and missing persons to have a single incident in common. But I digress. These three things gave us some early insight into how the Wilo people perceive the spirit world. There were three incidents; the first had to do with a jaguar.

"A jaguar broke into a house at the other end of the village last night," the man told me. He didn't seem overly concerned about it, practically yawning as he filled me in on some of the details. I knew the house he was referring to. It was a house that had long since passed its prime, and a determined toddler could have broken into it.

The presence of a jaguar in the vicinity wasn't too surprising either, since one of these big cats had already killed three village dogs several days before. What was surprising to me was the blasé attitude the Wilos had about it. I would have expected someone to organize a hunting party to track down the menacing animal, or to perhaps lure the jaguar into a trap. But no. No plans were being made to hunt the animal down. No one seemed too concerned that it might, for instance, kill someone. Hellooo! When I later asked others about that, I got vague shrugs.

"It ate a shirt," one villager explained to me. "Normal jaguars don't eat clothes. A witchdoctor from another tribe has sent this jaguar here."

I waited for further explanation but none was forthcoming. We would learn later that the spiritual beliefs of the Wilo people encourage a fatalistic attitude. If you are so unfortunate as to become the object of the wrath of a witchdoctor, there is little or nothing you can do about it. You passively accept your status as victim and make a mental note to not further offend the witchdoctor or evil spirits.

The second incident had to do with butterflies and clothes. For me, doing laundry in the jungle was a process. Separating lights from darks, delicates from normal, extra soiled from the nominally dirty is a challenge for many single guys, and I was no exception. But in the jungle that was the easy part. From there I had to carry it all down to the river and find a vacant rock, or a canoe turned upside down; this would be my washing machine. I would take one item at a time, wet it, rub some soap into it, and then, depending on whether it was extra soiled or nominally dirty, would either gently agitate it or savagely beat it against the washing machine. Then each item would be individually rinsed and examined for damages sustained in the washing process, and then wrung out by hand.

I would take the clothes back to an area in front of my house where I had strung a length of fish-line from one tree to another; this was my dryer. I would hang the clothes on the dryer and let Mother Nature do the rest.

One day I left my clothes out on the dryer for too long, and by evening, one of my neighbors – a short, wiry man named Lati – came over to my house. He was concerned about my clothes hanging on the line.

I had seen the Wilos themselves hanging their clothes out to dry. Sometimes they would string a vine between two points as a clothesline, and sometimes they would simply throw their clothes up onto their thatched roof to dry. What had escaped my notice, however, was that before nightfall, all clothes were taken into the house.

This is what Lati wanted to talk to me about. He had come to warn me about the danger of leaving my clothes out after dusk. It wasn't that someone might steal my clothes under the cover of darkness. It wasn't that it might rain and my clothes wouldn't dry properly. The danger was that evil spirits, in the form of butterflies, might land on my clothes during the night and leave a magical powder on them that would cause my skin to break out in a painful rash. It might even lead to my death.

Listening to Lati explain all of this to me, I realized I was being confronted with my first cultural dilemma. If I were to bring the clothes in at his request, I might be communicating that I too believed that leaving my clothes out overnight would cause me to fall victim to the evil spirits; that I too was afraid of this spiritual power. I didn't want Lati to think that.

On the other hand, if I were to ignore his advice and insist on leaving my clothes out all night, I might be communicating that I didn't care what Lati thought. It might discourage him and others from ever mentioning these sorts of things in the future. It possibly would communicate that I thought their beliefs were ridiculous; that I didn't care about what was important to them.

After Lati left, I went outside and brought the clothes in. I was careful from that time on to not leave my clothes out on the line after dark, not in order to avoid the power of the evil spirits, but to respect the wishes and beliefs of the tribal people. There would be plenty of time in the future to talk with them about this particular belief and to evaluate with them how it stacked up against the truths of the Bible. For now it was very important for the Wilo people to see that we wanted to understand their beliefs, and that we wouldn't ridicule them, nor take lightly their spiritual perspective of the world. We were the learners, they were our teachers.

The third thing that happened was that someone mysteriously went missing. A little boy had been swimming in the shallows of the river while his mother washed clothes nearby. One minute he was there, the next he was gone. Subsequent searches along the riverbanks turned up nothing.

The next day one of the men told me that evil spirits from downriver had taken the boy up in a whirlwind. He said the spirits usually take only girls. In this case they must have mistakenly thought the boy was a girl. It was likely, this man told me, that once the spirits realized their mistake, the unfortunate boy would be killed out of hand. The boy was never seen again, nor was his body ever recovered.

We were beginning to see a central element of the Wilo culture: fear. Fear is a dominant factor in every culture of the world. It is part of the human makeup. In the case of the Wilos, isolation and lack of knowledge had allowed the fear of malignant spiritual powers to become pervasive throughout practically every aspect of their lives.

The Bible claims that perfect love is the antidote for fear. We wished almost every day that we could tell the Wilo people about God's solution to their condition. We would have to be patient, though. The Wilos would have to continue exercising patience as well.

At times the temptation to get ahead of ourselves and begin teaching the Bible with our very limited language ability was overwhelming. Like a doctor who has a ready cure for a terminal disease and yet refuses to dispense it, it seemed almost criminal to keep silent. Nevertheless we were convinced that wait we must; that it would be negligent to begin attempting to dispense the gospel message at this early stage when miscommunication was certain. It would not be much different than the doctor dispensing his lifesaving medicine but failing to communicate the proper dosage and manner of administration.

Our hearts were broken on a regular basis as we witnessed the spiritual distress and despair of the Wilo people. They desperately wanted and needed to hear God's Word, and we were equally desperate to meet that need. But a barrier lay between us. We were living the experience of being so close and yet so far. We had little option but to continue dismantling that barrier piece by tiny piece, trusting that eventually this language could be learned, and God's Word could be clearly communicated.

Chapter 16

The Snake that Wanted to Snuggle

The benefits of rats and duct tape

It all began with a decidedly obnoxious rat. He was apparently of the conviction that what was mine was his, and he would often rummage through my stuff during the dark of night, noisily rustling plastic bags and knocking things over in his quest to find that perfect tasty morsel to eat. When he failed to find it there, he would scramble up into the thatched roof, gallop over to the rafters my hammock was strung from, and attempt to climb down my hammock ropes. I wasn't sure if he thought there was food in the hammock, or if he was simply irate and wanted to latch onto my toe to make me pay for keeping the food supplies closed up so tightly.

Whatever his intent in wishing to climb into the hammock with me, I was adamantly opposed. Whenever I felt the tiny vibration of his feet on the rope, I would shine the flashlight and he would scurry off. Some nights I would get up and try to hunt him down, but he was very skilled in evasive tactics.

One morning, after yet another night of fitful sleep sandwiched between small skirmishes with the rat, I had had enough. I unpacked a few rat traps and baited them with little pieces of banana, placing them strategically about the house. There, Rat. Come and get your tasty morsels now.

That night, he again attempted to walk down the hammock ropes and again I chased him away. I dozed off only to be awakened a short time later by a loud snap. Groggily, I leaped out of the hammock, a difficult maneuver to execute even when fully awake. Heart pounding, I stood for a moment while I processed the sound. The rat trap! I shined the flashlight in that direction, and sure enough, the rat had gotten his tasty morsel, and it appeared it wouldn't be his last meal, either; I had just fallen victim to an eat and run. I sensed I was being mocked.

For several weeks we continued engrossed in this macabre chess match; the difference between he and I was that he seemed to enjoy it. However, I was determined that he would not conquer the hammock, at least not with me in it. I sprayed the ropes with bug repellant, but that discomfited me more than him. I sacrificed two pie plates for the cause, punching a hole in the middle of each one and threading the hammock ropes through them in order to block off access to the hammock. This strategy backfired in that it did little more than give the rat something else with which to make noise in the middle of the night.

In desperation, I dug out my precious roll of duct tape. I wrapped the hammock ropes with it, sticky side out. I felt good about this plan. The rat would start down the rope, step on the sticky substance, and would either retreat, or else become ensnared in the tape, like a fly in a spider's web. I preferred the latter scenario.

It was during this time that a couple of veteran missionaries arrived to help us evaluate the progress we had been making in language and culture study. They were very curious to know why I had pie plates and duct tape on my hammock ropes, and they laughed when I explained about the obnoxious rat. Their laughter diminished somewhat when they learned that they would be swinging their hammocks in my house that night. No, I didn't have any more pie plates. Yes, I could spare a little duct tape.

Late that night, I was awakened by an unfamiliar crinkling sound. I remained still for a few seconds, trying to determine what it might be. I eventually got up and with the flashlight looked around but saw nothing. As I returned to the corner of the house that was my bedroom, the light caught a slight movement on my hammock rope. My heart leapt! Was it finally checkmate for the rat?

I rushed to the rope, prepared to deliver a death blow, but froze when I saw that it was not the rat. The heebie-jeebies were definitely in order. I backed away, staring at the snake, until I realized it wasn't going anywhere. Even with a pair of pliers it was difficult to extract the snake from the sticky embrace of the duct tape. In the process, I accidentally crushed its head... four or five times.

By this time, one of the visiting missionaries had awakened and sleepily asked, "What's going on?"

"Ummm, not much. Just a snake that was wanting to snuggle." I took the snake outside. My hands were trembling so much that I could barely muster the strength to throw it into the bushes. Have I mentioned that I really do have a high level of antipathy toward snakes?

I have no idea where the rat was during this entire episode. For all I know, he had put the snake up to it and was in the corner chortling as the scene unfolded. In any event, it was the rat that had driven me to put the duct tape on the ropes, so I guess I owed him a debt of gratitude. Thanks, Rat. Now, might I interest you in one of these tasty morsels of banana?

Chapter 17

The Burial Procession

A small girl's death reminds the missionary why he is there

Through blurry eyes one morning, I noted fewer children than usual staring in at me. I saw people walking down toward the north side of the village, so I made my way down to that end as well. A limping gazelle walking through a den of hungry lions wouldn't have received as many stares as I did as I strolled past the houses.

There was a stream of people heading out of the village, and several of the men indicated that I should come with them, so I inserted myself into the current and was swept along toward the base of a nearby hill. I saw that several people in the front of the procession were carrying a section of an old dugout canoe. And looking at some of the sad and concerned faces around me, it didn't require a Sherlock moment to conclude that this was a funeral procession. A girl had died during the night while I had slept oblivious, and many of the Wilos had stayed up all night with the girl's body to watch over her spirit.

One thing every culture of the world has to deal with is death. Some societies cremate the dead, some grind the dead person's bones into a powder and mix it into a drink. Others tie the dead person into a chair, or up in a tree. The Wilos bury their dead. In the past they would sometimes place the bodies of important people inside caves, but that was no longer the practice.

As the procession made its way to the base of the hill, I was struck by the relatively light atmosphere among those present.

There was no wailing, there was no subdued sobbing. Certainly there were somber expressions, a few teary eyes, but there was also murmured conversation and even occasional laughter.

We arrived at a small clearing a short way up the hill to find several young men who were finishing their work of digging the grave. They smiled and jumped out of the hole as we walked up. Everybody gathered around the grave in a loose circle. Someone searched around in the nearby bushes and came back cradling four large rocks in his arms. He set them down by the grave, jumped into the hole, and placed a rock in each corner where the crude casket was to be placed. Others standing around seemed to be giving him instructions, and when everybody was satisfied with the placement of the four rocks, he climbed back out.

Several people then addressed their attention toward the casket. They made hand motions and spoke among themselves; it looked as though they were making sure that the casket was facing the proper direction. We were to later learn that it is important for the Wilos to bury their dead in such a manner that the feet of the corpse be pointing eastward, toward the rising sun. Should some hapless corpse be buried facing the wrong direction, entry into the afterlife would be complicated and the spirit of the dead person would be more likely to wander, and thus interfere with the lives of the living.

At the time, though, I knew nothing of this. I stood off from the main crowd as several men gently lowered the casket into the grave. An incredible sadness pressed down upon me. The girl's body was encased in the dugout canoe that served as a casket, and dirt was about to be filled in around her. Over the next few years her flesh would slowly revert back to dirt, and yet in a real sense she would continue to live on.

Since as far back as the 1970s these people had been waiting with great desire and anticipation to hear God's Word. Twenty years later, and here they were, still living and dying without that opportunity. How many more would die before we gained fluency in their language?

A line was formed by those attending this burial, and one by one they took their turn at stepping up to the grave and scooping several shovelfuls of dirt back into the hole. Even the small children participated, some reluctantly, others with great enthusiasm. And so the simple casket was covered, the grave filled, and the book closed on the short earthly life of this Wilo girl. But through her death God planted a renewed sense of urgency in my heart that day, an urgency to be about the business of learning the Wilo language as soon as possible, so that a clear gospel message could be introduced into their world. The clock was ticking.

For their part, the Wilos were convinced that having their own missionaries now, they wouldn't have to wait much longer to finally hear the message they had so been longing for. I would, they assumed, be speaking their language perfectly in three or four months. Their language was so simple that even the little village children could speak it.

I was reluctant to inform them that their optimism had met its match, or rather its nemesis, in their new missionary. I knew that it would take me at least three or four years of intense study and practice to learn this language fluently. For his part, God was silent on this issue of how many years it would take, a silence for which I am grateful in retrospect.

Chapter 18

A Grubby Hand

A friendly neighbor offers a squirming, juicy snack

Buchi came over to visit with a bunch of other guys in tow. He had a mischievous gleam in his eyes, a gleam indicating he was greatly anticipating the next few minutes. I wondered what was up.

He didn't keep me in suspense for long. He strode across the room, extended his palm toward me and, with a smile said, "Do you eat these?"

Do you eat these? A simple question, fairly straightforward and without a lot of ambiguity. Nevertheless, I found it to be a question more easily asked than answered. If I had been on the witness stand and Buchi had been the prosecutor, it would have gone something like this:

"Well, Mr Jank, do you?"

"Ummm..."

"Come now, Mr Jank. The question is not so difficult to answer. Do – you – eat – these?"

"Well, the thing is, is that sometimes..."

"Really, a simple yes or no will suffice."

"Yeah, no. It's just that..."

"Your Honor, this defendant obviously has no taste for these proceedings. May it please the court...?"

"Indeed. Please answer the question, Mr Jank," the judge would smirk.

"Uh, what was the question again?" And Buchi would once again extend his opened hand toward me, palm up, and say, "Mr Jank, do you eat these?"

"Do you mean, would I like to eat them, or am I willing to eat them, or have I eaten them in the past, or..."

But we weren't in a court of law, and I had not sworn to say the truth, the whole truth, and nothing but the truth. I smiled delightedly, and said, "*Ha-oh.*"

Having precipitously committed to this course of action, my eyes frantically searched out the smallest from among the grubs as I enthusiastically blurted, "Let me try one." I tried emphasizing the word *one*, but to no avail, as Buchi dumped four into my hand. Tim happened to be in the house as well, and I smiled encouragingly at him as he received the same treatment. We both tried one. The others we set aside to be savored later and somehow, inexplicably, they managed to escape into the garbage can. Very crafty, those grubs.

Buchi and I had become friends almost immediately upon my arrival in Pakali. During my first days in the village when everybody looked like clones of one another, he was easily distinguishable because of his bright neon-colored shorts and his wide grin that, although sadly lacking in pearly whites, was infectious and engaging. The missing teeth and a bump on his wrist were compliments of a fall he took from a tree a few years back. One night he recounted to me how he had been in pretty bad shape and had almost died, but his grandfather had chanted and done witchcraft to make him better.

His house, a circular mud wall with a thatched roof rising to a sharp point, was only a few paces from my own, and he often came over to talk in his very limited Spanish or to simply sit and watch me. Sometimes he would accept a cup of coffee, although he maybe liked it as much as I did his grubs. Our conversation topics ranged from the giants that live on the grasslands north of the village to his younger brother's death from a venomous snake bite; from what it's like eight hours upriver to what it's like in North America.

His interest in learning about the Bible had motivated him to acquire three New Testaments – none, of course, in his own language. He told me that when he could learn more of God's

Word he would travel to neighboring villages to tell others about the things he was learning.

Buchi, like many others in the Wilo tribe, was very anxious to learn what the Bible had to say. He would ask questions, but because of the language barrier, we were incapable of answering most of them. For now, our lives would have to do all the talking.

We were objects of much curiosity. Every day there seemed to be a steady stream of people stopping by to observe us. It didn't matter that we were often involved in mundane activities like eating, or studying, or working – it was all fascinating to them. They would stare at us up close and from a distance, in groups and as individuals.

Our lives were being thoroughly read, thoroughly scrutinized and analyzed through a cultural filter of which we were still largely ignorant. We were constantly being challenged with the thought – what do these people see when they look at us? Do they see us as people who are reputable in conduct? Are we available and approachable, or do we seem to care primarily about ourselves? Are we friendly? Are we willing and wanting to be taught by the people around us?

A foundation of first impressions was being laid. This foundation would affect the relationships that were to be built over the coming years, relationships that were already being formed between us and the Wilo people.

Chapter 19

The Problem with a Little Knowledge

Sorry seems to be the hardest word

Language learning at times required that we brush up on our thespian skills, such as they were. After we had embarked upon our most excellent language learning adventure, there came the day when we realized we needed to know how to apologize in the Wilo language. Tim and I would often play soccer with the Wilo guys and in the process we would sometimes bump into one of them, or trip one of them up. We wanted to know how to say "I'm sorry" or "Excuse me".

We tried eliciting the phrase using Spanish, but no one knew what we were talking about. We realized we would have to establish a scene, and paint a picture.

Tim and I took advantage of a time when a group of Wilos were gathered in my house. We told them we wanted to ask them something, and then proceeded to elaborately enact a soccer scene in which we both attempted to gain possession of the ball and, in the process, I knocked Tim down. Tim did a great job of falling to the ground dramatically in slow motion. I looked on with much concern and consternation.

We felt we had done a pretty decent job of it, although if we'd had time to prepare more fully, we perhaps would have included a sound track, not to mention a speech thanking the Academy. Our Wilo audience appreciated the performance nonetheless, chuckling as Tim crumpled to the ground.

As Tim lay there, I pointed to him and asked the spectators, "What would I say now about this that happened? What would you say?"

There was silence. I was glad to see they were putting some thought into their answer. Heaven forbid that I would go around saying the wrong thing each time I attempted to apologize for something.

The Wilos huddled together and discussed it among themselves. We understood very little of what they were saying, and were relieved when they finally came to a consensus. "*Omona toato*," they said. "We would say, '*Omona toato*' when something like that happens."

Tim and I frantically wrote down the phrase in our ever-present notebooks. Being a true-blue Canadian, I in particular was tickled pink to finally know how to apologize for my many offenses. We were quite pleased with our success and from that time forward didn't hesitate to enthusiastically apologize at any possible opportunity in order to practice this new phrase. Our apologies were met with varying responses, ranging from hearty laughter to puzzled silence.

As the days passed into months and we gained more knowledge of the Wilo language, we made a disturbing discovery. Much to our chagrin and confoundment, it suddenly became clear to us that we had yet again fallen victim to miscommunication. The phrase the Wilos had given us months earlier was not an apology at all. Apparently our acting debut had not been as convincing as we had assumed. Misunderstanding the point of the skit, the Wilos had given us not an apology, but rather an observation. We discovered the Wilo word *omona* meant "simply", or "on purpose". The word *toato* meant "he tripped". The phrase in its entirety could be translated "He just tripped on purpose."

All this time, our effusive apologies had meant nothing more than that. "Oh, did I step on your foot? He just fell on purpose," we would say apologetically. "Was that your little seedling I ran over with the lawn-mower? He just fell on purpose."

I wanted nothing more than to immediately go around to all the people I had "apologized" to over the past months and apologize for not apologizing. Unfortunately, the Wilo language didn't have an apology word or phrase. As much as it went against my nature and culture, I would have to get used to not apologizing, at least verbally.

This little episode in my new life as a language and culture learner reminded me that sometimes a little knowledge can be a dangerous thing. Just when I thought I knew how to apologize, I knew nothing of the sort. It wasn't until I had gained more fluency in the language that I was able to recognize the errors that contaminated my understanding.

It didn't take us long to realize that the Wilos also were falling victim to the same dangers of a little knowledge, although in a much more serious context. Over the years, they had gained a little knowledge of God's Word; bits and pieces of fact and fiction they had picked up here and there. For instance, they "knew" that God and Satan were at one time of equal power. They "knew" that Satan is God's ambassador of evil to this world. They "knew" that Cain was the physical offspring of Satan and Eve. Their bits of knowledge were obviously creating more confusion than enlightenment.

A question the Wilos asked us quite often was, "When are you going to begin teaching God's Word to us?" They knew that was what we were working toward, and they were anxious to hear. Recognizing the misconceptions the Wilos had of the Bible motivated us to press forward in both language study and culture investigation. God's Word presented in a clear and understandable manner was what would clear up these kinds of misunderstandings; God's Word was what would explain God's truth. A great way to combat the inaccuracies of a little knowledge is to provide a fuller knowledge. Each step we took toward language fluency and cultural understanding was one step closer the Wilos came to hearing and understanding God's Word.

Chapter 20

Witchdoctor Appointment

A witchdoctor refers his patient to the ophthalmologist

The typical Wilo grows up to be resistant to pain. Not that it doesn't hurt when they stub their toe or when an errant fish-hook sinks into their flesh. They just don't react to the extent that we normally would. It's not unusual, for instance, for a Wilo man to stitch himself up when an axe or machete inadvertently splits open his foot. He washes out the wound, threads some line through the eye of a fish-hook and has a go at it. No big deal. Doctors do it all the time.

So when Pancham, one of the village leaders, stopped by the house to tell me his eye was really sore, I believed him. It appeared normal except for some local swelling, and he said it was sensitive to light and wind. None of us missionaries were nurses or doctors, and there was little we could do for him. There was a government-paid medic assigned to Pakali, but between vacation time and trips out to town to collect his paycheck, he was not often around. Today was no exception.

Which left us with three choices. We could ignore Pancham's medical problem, we could get on the radio and call in an evacuation flight, or we could wait until an airplane was scheduled to come in and evacuate him on that flight.

The first option wasn't really an option at all. The second option was the most drastic. Calling in an emergency evacuation flight was quite expensive, and it played havoc with the existing flight schedule of the airplanes. The pilots were always ready and willing to respond, but we didn't want to be calling in emergency flights unnecessarily.

In the case of Pancham we decided that the next time the mission plane came in we would see if there was room for him to fly to town in order to get his eye examined. It didn't seem like an emergency, and he agreed.

The next morning someone stopped by the house and informed me that Pancham planned to go to a village downriver to see a witchdoctor about his eye problem. Later that day, when I went down to the river to get my daily bath, Pancham and his wife were bathing as well. I asked him if his eye still hurt and he said yes, it did. I asked him if he was going to go see the witchdoctor and, a little hesitantly, he said he was. I said, "Well, let me know what the witchdoctor says."

A few days later Pancham was back and sitting across from me at my table. We were drinking coffee and talking about this and that. His eye was almost swollen shut and it was obviously causing some pain. I politely ignored it for a while, but eventually curiosity got the better of me.

"So, how did it go?" I asked. "How did your visit to the witchdoctor go?"

"It still hurts," he said, referring to his eye.

Yes, I could see that. What I was curious to learn was what the witchdoctor had done. Did he perform some special ceremony? Did he dramatically throw dust in the air, or stomp his feet, or attempt to suck a sickness spirit out of Pancham? Did he chant? Dance?

I contented myself though with asking, "What did the witchdoctor say? Did he find a cure?"

"He didn't find a cure," Pancham responded. "He just gave me some water to put in my eye and told me to go see an eye doctor in town as soon as possible."

What? What kind of a witchdoctor was that! It made me wonder if this witchdoctor maybe had a medical manual tucked away somewhere in his thatched-roof hut. Fortunately, Pancham decided to follow his witchdoctor's advice and soon went off to see an eye doctor. I could just imagine him walking into the doctor's office in town.

Doctor: "Good morning, Mr... uh," he looks down at the sheet of paper on his desk, "Mr Pancham. What brings you here today?"

Pancham: "Well, doctor, it's my eye. It's very sore."

Doctor: "OK. I'm sure we can fix you up just fine. Did someone refer you to me?"

Pancham: "Yes, as a matter of fact, the old witchdoctor who lives on the Balawa River, the one who lives down a bend from the mouth of the Yebera tributary, he suggested I come see you."

Doctor: "Oh yes! How is my old friend doing? We were in medical school together years ago, but he dropped out to pursue a career in shamanism. How is he?"

Pancham: "Not bad."

Doctor: "Well, give him my greetings. Have a seat and I'll be right with you."

But it probably didn't happen quite like that. I never did learn the details of his visit to the eye doctor in town. What I do know is that when he returned he still had a sore eye, but with time it got better and he suffered no lasting damage to it.

Chapter 21

Roach Busters

A most unpleasant awakening

If they knocked, I certainly didn't hear it. The doors were still locked, the sun was just beginning to peek over the horizon, and I had no idea I was not alone in the house.

The roosters outside my window, after a long night of enthusiastic crowing, had finally convinced me I might as well get up, if for no other reason than to throw sticks and stones at them. Had I been more in tune with rooster language I might have recognized their crowing to be something more than obnoxious noise pollution. As it was, their heroic desperate warnings of an impending and swiftly approaching invasion fell only on irritable and unappreciative ears.

I reluctantly swung my feet out of the hammock, stood up and transitioned directly into my daily zombie imitation, destination: coffee pot.

Not long ago, with the help of a few energetic visitors, we had poured a concrete floor in my house, and now my bare feet padded on the cold floor as I made my bleary-eyed way to the kitchen. Oblivious to the baleful gaze of the silent intruders, I lit the propane stove and heated up some left-over coffee from the day before. I poured myself a cup, and with the wafting aroma came also the uncomfortable sense that all was not right with the world.

My eyes finally focused on the floor and immediately, if not somewhat frantically, I transitioned into my Fred Astaire impersonation, destination: outside. I was halfway to the door before I realized I was in fact in no immediate danger. I stopped and, with my feet once again resting easy on the floor, took stock of the situation.

These home invaders I had seen before. Their silent, unannounced arrivals rarely failed to give me an adrenaline rush. Perhaps in reference to some obscure past affiliation with the Soviet military, they're known as red army ants. They were streaming into the house from every nook and cranny, marching eight abreast and criss-crossing the walls and floor.

I contemplated engaging them in battle; they had, after all, invaded my home. However, I began to feel more kindly disposed toward them when I saw they weren't particularly interested in inflicting bodily harm on my person. They seemed to be saying to me, "Just mind your own business, Bud, and you won't get hurt."

That was probably good advice. I remembered in our last confrontation I had inflicted a great many casualties upon a similar red army but had in the end been overwhelmed and undone by their sheer numbers. The bitter taste of defeat had been almost nauseating. Curiously, it was a taste not unlike that of inhaling too much air saturated with "Raid".

No. Past experience had taught me that resistance was futile. Fleeing was unnecessary. I knew what this situation called for: it called for another cup of coffee, since my first cup had spilled onto my clothes and across the floor. I refilled my coffee cup, tiptoed my way back to the hammock and focused on minding my own business.

For the next couple of hours I entertained myself by watching the ants search through the house, rounding up cockroaches and other bugs and whisking them away. Somehow, in all their searching, they missed a dead bug that was at the foot of the bookcase. I pushed it toward one of the columns of ants, and one of their scouts rushed over to investigate. A crowd quickly gathered around the dead bug, and they obligingly hefted it up and carried it away, although with a noted lack of appreciation for my help and participation. I must admit, however, they seemed to be doing a good job of cleaning up the house, taking the creepy-crawlies while leaving everything else intact.

Then, as quickly and quietly as they had come, they left. I didn't notice them leaving; it just seemed like one minute they were there, and the next they were gone. The coast being clear, I hesitantly returned to the kitchen, afraid of what I might find or not find. I rounded the black plastic sheet that was my wall and a wave of disappointment swept over me as the scene in the kitchen greeted my eyes. I guess I had been overly optimistic. Apparently they don't do dishes.

Chapter 22

Acceptance Is...

Signs that indicate acceptance into Wilo society

We sort of stumbled into acceptance. It happened almost without us noticing it, much less attempting to cultivate it.

My mind takes me back to an encounter I had with a small village boy a few days after my arrival in Pakali. I was making my way up a small trail, a leafy wall of grass and shrubs rising up on both sides. I rounded a corner and a little boy, sans clothing, was walking toward me, oblivious of my approach.

I had a prescient feeling that when tall, white stranger met small, Wilo child on a trail that left little room for evasive maneuvering, small Wilo child would morph into a hollering, quickly disappearing cloud of dust.

In the jungle, barefooted children learn at an early age the benefits of keeping a sharp eye on the trail, and this lad was jungle through and through. He was studiously looking down at his feet as he closed in, which dismayed me in that I had little doubt the force of his reaction would be in direct proportion to the distance between us.

Perhaps I should clear my throat, I thought belatedly. I knew that any attempt on my part now to calm or allay his concern would only exacerbate his panic. I simply braced myself for our impending meeting.

The boy looked up from the trail, only to find his gaze filled with *moi*. He came to an abrupt stop. His jaw dropped lower and lower, his eyes grew wider and wider. He filled his lungs to capacity, paused briefly as though to add to the suspense, and then let out a terrified scream that many a Hollywood producer would pay good money for. Thanks, kid. It's nice to meet you, too.

Then he decided that distance was more desirable than pointless histrionics, and proceeded to beat a speedy retreat back to his mom, who was standing in a doorway laughing as she observed this moving interaction between the new missionary and her son. Certainly not a preferred introduction, but more or less to be expected.

As the months went by I noticed small changes indicating that a better, more relaxed acceptance of us by the Wilo people was developing. For starters, children no longer ran away screaming whenever I approached, although they still often ran away. But that was progress.

In the early days, whenever I would walk through the village, all eyes would follow my every move. It often made me feel like a lonely gunfighter in the Wild West, walking down an empty, dusty street while from the houses people peeked furtively through the windows and doorways. I was relieved to notice that with the passing of time, I became less of a spectacle and more a normal part of the environment.

Something else that made it painfully clear I was gaining acceptance into mainstream Wilo society was that I would get kicked in the shins as hard as the next guy while playing soccer, and everybody would laugh about it just as loudly as with anyone else. Who knew acceptance could be so hurtful? Perhaps I would have to invest in some shin guards.

None of the Wilo people had any kind of running water in their houses, so they would spend quite a bit of time at the river. Most bathed there once or twice a day. They would scrub their clothes and wash their dishes there, and they would do these things in various states of undress. Of course, whenever the new missionary showed up unannounced at the river, everybody would scramble madly to put on their shorts, or slip into a shirt.

Over time, these scramblings became less pronounced, and eventually the Wilos became comfortable maintaining their own cultural standards of modesty whether the missionary was present or not. This was another sign that we were being accepted into society.

In general, the Wilos were a very hospitable people. They would often proffer a snack or a tin plate of food to us when we were out in the jungle with them or in their homes. For our part, we made a concerted effort to accept this generosity with enthusiasm, no matter the content. Rarely were we served something distasteful to us.

This feeding of the missionaries was initially a spectator activity. People would gather around to watch us eat their food. They would lean over and whisper to one another, make comments, laugh, and ask us slowly and with exaggerated enunciation if we liked it. For someone who prefers being unnoticed and out of the spotlight, this treatment was quite excruciating. Thankfully, the scrutiny became much less pronounced as the Wilos began accepting us more fully into their world.

From day one we had made an effort to communicate that we were not special or important people. The important thing was the message we hoped to communicate to them. As the Wilos continued seeing that we were not there to pass judgment on their lifestyle and culture, that we had no interest in imposing our standards and opinions and beliefs on their society, acceptance followed naturally.

We desired to live among them in simplicity and sincerity, and on our good days that's how it was. God didn't have us there just so he could do a work among the Wilos; he wanted to continue molding and forming each of us into vessels that would honor and glorify him. God had his work cut out for him.

Chapter 23

Campaign Candy

A boat ride to a nearby village results in some candy
which results in the worst kind of sinking sensation

Several of the Wilos came by the house one day to invite us
missionaries to travel with them to a village downriver. Tim and I
took them up on the invitation. It would be a perfect opportunity
not only to spend some time with these particular Wilos, but also
to get out and about, and get to know some of the Wilos in the
village of Poleni. My neighbor Yachi had a small outboard motor
that would be mounted onto a dugout canoe, so we'd be traveling
in style.

I don't remember anything about our trip down to Poleni. Nor
do I remember what we did while spending the day there. What I
do remember is what happened on our way back. Yachi was
steering the boat, keeping it within a stone's throw of the
riverbank. The outboard motor was gamely pushing the heavy
dugout canoe upstream, slowly but surely.

Suddenly, up ahead we saw a large speedboat, and it was
approaching fast. We expected it to pass by us, and were
preparing to cut across its substantial wake in order to prevent the
waves from breaching our canoe and sending us to the murky
bottom of the river. None of us wanted that to happen.

We breathed a collective sigh of relief when we realized the
speedboat was slowing down as it neared us. We wouldn't have to
contend with the waves after all. The speedboat pulled up
alongside our canoe. One of the passengers in it was a local
politician whose constituents included the tribal people living

along the banks of the Balawa River.

He talked to us a bit in Spanish, taking the opportunity to campaign extemporaneously for re-election. As he talked, he reached into a bag and tossed over a piece of candy to each of us, a campaign tactic not uncommon among the politicians of that area. Many thanks, Mr Mayor.

He was quite friendly and chatty, but had a long way to travel before nightfall. Pushing away from us, the driver of the speedboat gave his motor full throttle and away they went, leaving us in their wake. This ended up being something of a problem for us.

Yachi put his motor in gear as well and we started out, but he was distracted with getting his piece of candy out of the wrapper. He didn't notice the swell created by the departed speedboat. First one wave, and then another crashed over our canoe.

Many things were said, many feelings animatedly expressed during those few slow-motion seconds. We knew we were going down. Yachi desperately pointed the canoe toward the riverbank and gunned the engine in a heroic attempt to reach the safety of the shore. Alas, it was not to be. Too much water had poured into the canoe. We were about four meters from the bank when our forward motion ceased and our downward motion began in earnest.

We all had time to grab a few items before the dugout was pulled from under us by the clutches of the deep. Then we struggled toward the riverbank, fought our way through the brambles lining the river, and reached out for dry land. The speedboat was disappearing in the distance; no help would be forthcoming from that source. Thanks again, Mr Mayor.

Everybody was laughing as we pulled ourselves up out of the river. Even Yachi, who owned the outboard motor that now rested somewhere beneath the surface, seemed mildly amused. It was hard to extinguish the Wilo sense of humor, and it was impossible not to join in the laughter.

We decided to dive down and attempt to raise the canoe to the surface again. Fortunately the water was shallow enough that we were eventually able to disconnect the outboard motor and drag it up onto dry ground. And with a bit more work the canoe once again floated on the surface of the water.

We dried out the motor as best we could, and an hour later we were back in business, continuing our trip home to Pakali. I didn't know just where Mr Mayor stood on many of the political issues of the day, but I did know this: his chances of garnering our votes were now laid to rest in a cold watery grave where his campaign candy had sent us.

Chapter 24

Nightmare on Sesame Street

The Wilos' counting system would send the Count to the psychiatrist's couch

Television wasn't a big part of my childhood, but on those occasions when I had the opportunity to watch a show or two, I would often tune in to a children's show called *Sesame Street*. One of the characters on that show was the Count, a Dracula lookalike who *loved* to count anything and everything.

I don't think the Count would have enjoyed the Wilo language at all. His manner of counting, after all, was very simplistic and one-dimensional. He would use the numbers one through ten to count people, and then would turn around and use those very same numbers to count balloons. How lame is that!

Had he ever been tasked with counting in the Wilo language, methinks the good Count would have suffered nightmares and cold sweats for the rest of his television career.

I myself never did all that well in math class, but one thing that made it tolerable was the fact that the word "three", for instance, is used to describe the sum total of any particular item equaling three. Thus, when there are three stones, I can confidently state that the sum total of stones is three. And when there are three trees, I can, with equal confidence, state that the sum total of trees is three. As long as there are three of something, the number word used to describe the quantity is three.

That's pretty nice, and very convenient. That is the counting system the Count and I, and probably you, are familiar with. The Wilo language, not surprisingly, went about counting in a very different manner.

In the Wilo language, numbers don't exist in isolation. It's impossible to count from one to ten in a generic manner. Built into the number itself is a clue as to what is being counted.

What do I mean by that? Well, let me break it down for you. In the Wilo language, every noun is assigned a group for it to belong to, usually based upon the shape or properties of the object. Round things form one group, flat things form another, long skinny things another, pointy things another, sharp things yet another. There are well over a dozen such distinct groupings of nouns, otherwise known as noun classes.

Each of these noun classes is identified by a specific sound that represents that particular attribute, and these representative sounds attach themselves to the end of all of the nouns in that group. Round things, for example, are assigned the sound *po*. Using English, it would look like this: ballpo, marblepo, eggpo. Long skinny things get the sound *bo*, like bananabo, hosebo, ropebo. Sharp things get the sound *pi*, like shovelpi, knifepi, razorpi.

You're still with me, right? Just checking, because it's about to get good.

In the Wilo language a number isn't a number unless it includes one of those noun class suffixes. There is no way to count just for the sake of counting. The language requires that an object, or at least a specific noun class, be in focus when counting. Embedded in the number itself is a clue as to the shape or attribute of the object you're counting, and that clue is the suffix assigned to that particular noun class.

Did I just say it's a suffix? My bad. It often is a suffix, but at times it gets embedded into the middle of the number, so sometimes it's an infix. Thankfully, it is never a prefix.

Anyway, what I'm trying to say, and what you're trying to comprehend, is that the word for each number changes when you switch from one noun class to another. You can't use the same numbers to count cockroaches that you would use to count pancakes, for instance. They are in separate groupings of nouns...

unless, of course, the cockroach has just made a mad dash across the floor and has wound up on the receiving end of a blunt instrument, in which case you could conceivably transfer the remains of the cockroach into the pancake class.

Basically, what it boils down to is this: each noun class uses its own exclusive variation of the numbers for counting. Because the Wilo language has more than a dozen distinct noun classes, this means there are more than a dozen different ways to say "three".

Pretty nifty, huh? "Hooray, English!" the Count blurts out enthusiastically.

I can't blame him. I would hate to teach a math class in the Wilo language. I mean, you know something's a tad bizarre when it takes several pages just to explain how to count. I bet you can't wait for me to explain how these same noun class specifiers are also woven into adjectives and other parts of speech, but lest I be accused of inflicting cruel and unusual treatment upon innocent readers, I shall desist.

But I cannot in good conscience let you go without first explaining about the root meanings of the Wilo numbers. It is a counting system based on the digits of a person's hands and feet. Perhaps you would picture it better if you hold out your hand in a fist and then uncurl each finger as it is mentioned. Are you ready?

The word one is "the thumb". The word two is "the index finger". Three is "the summit finger". Four is "the middle finger". And five is "one hand". Pretty straightforward.

The word six is "the other hand and the thumb". Seven is "the other hand and the index finger". You can guess what eight and nine are, right? And ten is "two hands".

From there we move downward to the feet, but I won't ask you to take your shoes and socks off. Eleven is "from the downriver hand the thumb". Twelve is "from the downriver hand the index finger". Thirteen is "from the downriver hand the summit finger", and so on.

It starts getting very cumbersome when you get past fifteen, which is "from the downriver hand one hand". Sixteen is "from the downriver hand the other hand and the thumb". Seventeen is "from the downriver hand the other hand and the index finger". Eighteen is "from the downriver hand the other hand and the summit finger". Nineteen is "from the downriver hand the other hand and the middle finger". And finally, twenty is "from the downriver hand two hands".

Whew! Add to the mix the need to include the correct noun class specifier, and you've got yourself quite a challenge. When asked to count beyond twenty, most Wilos usually became confused about how to proceed, although the more determined ones would sometimes continue with "one person and the thumb..."

What do these numbers look like in the Wilo language? Well, if the Count of *Sesame Street* were to count knives in the Wilo language, he would first have to know that knives are in the *pi* class of nouns, then he would start by saying "*Bakwapi*," which means one sharp thing. To say seven, he would say, "*Hele-muthodopilataha*." To say thirteen he would say, "*Alinosamu-thowapopikwa*." And were he to say nineteen he would say, "*Alinosamuthohelemuthoo'wehemuhawaopi*." So, can you see the noun classifier in each of those words?

So for us, the counting system of the Wilo language was a challenge to decipher, and tedious to use. Even the Wilos themselves found it cumbersome. Well before we missionaries arrived on the scene, many Wilos had begun familiarizing themselves with the counting system of Spanish, where "one" means "one", no matter what you're counting. That was OK by me.

Chapter 25

Grandpa's Double Trouble

One of the twins must die

Her grandpa was a big man, and strong. He had a sturdy build, like a beer keg with arms and legs. He could walk for hours through the jungle carrying seventy pounds of garden produce, and yet was agile enough to shimmy up tall trees and then slide back down with a stalk of palm fruit in hand.

He was one of the few men in the village who had more than one wife. He tended to live in his own orbit, not fully a part of the village social life, but not completely separate from it either. He always seemed to have a ready smile and polite conversation; a pleasant sort of guy.

That was the grandpa she would have gotten to know if only things had not gone so horribly wrong. As it was, her grandpa was intent on ending her young life. She had been born into this world just a few hours earlier and now plans were being made for her life to be taken from her.

I don't think her grandpa really wanted to do it, but he had little choice in the matter. Everybody knew that when twins were born, drastic measures had to be taken to protect society. For the good of the community, one, if not both of the newborn twins must die.

The young mother who had just given birth wanted to kill both babies, but grandpa had intervened and said that only one need die. He wasn't a heartless, sadistic man. That wasn't it at all. It was just that, with the newborn's father being away, well, someone had to take charge. Someone had to make the tough decision to do what was best for everybody. So, this baby girl had to die. Everybody knew that.

The afterbirth of his newborn granddaughter had not been cleaned off. She had immediately become an object of fear and revulsion, set aside unattended while the mother concerned herself with her twin sister. This wasn't a good situation. Twins were not a good omen. If no one were willing to adopt this unwanted baby and take her far from the village, then grandpa stood ready to do his duty and solve the problem in the same grisly manner that Wilos had been employing for generations. Strangulation was how these things had been taken care of in the past. His brown eyes searched out a length of vine that would serve the purpose, his expression grim but determined.

The birth of twins is trouble in many tribal cultures; the Wilos were no exception. Now that twin girls had been born, it was unthinkable that the mother would keep both of them. If no one intervened, the unwanted child would be perfunctorily put to death. The clock was ticking; there was little time to waste.

Fear had raised its ugly head. Fear was going to be the death of this innocent baby girl. Several of the Wilos begged us missionaries to take the baby and save her life. They didn't want the child to die, but the rules of their society were very clear; culturally their hands were tied.

To what extent should we get involved in this? We really didn't know. We could do what these Wilos were asking and rescue the baby from her imminent death, but doing so might well compromise our future in the village. The Wilos might later insist the child be taken away from the village and raised elsewhere. Or perhaps they would blame the taboo child (and by association us) for any sickness and misfortune that might befall the village in the future. Should we jeopardize our ministry among the Wilos in order to save this baby's life?

Another option was to tell the Wilos that they shouldn't kill the baby. Maybe they would listen to us and decide to risk allowing the baby to live among them. But we weren't there to impose our own moral standards on the tribal people. We were not an authority in their lives to be dictating what they should or shouldn't do. They had invited us to live in their village, not to tell them how to act, but rather to tell them about God's Talk.

A third option was to simply not interfere. We could stand back and do nothing while the life of this newborn baby was snuffed out practically right in front of our eyes. But that didn't seem right, either. We were torn.

Fortunately, before we had to choose any of those options, visitors from a neighboring tribe arrived and agreed to take the baby girl. Her life was spared, and grandpa was relieved to not have to carry through with his grisly duty.

Have you heard of two men named Perez and Zerah? The Bible says that they were twins born to Judah and Tamar. What about Jacob and Esau? They were twins, too, and the Bible has much to say about them.

What would the Wilos think about these twins? Would they assume that because they were twins, they might actually have been evil spirits? Would they think that these twins should have been put to death immediately upon being born? Would they conclude that the conflict between Jacob and Esau was a direct result of one of them being an evil spirit?

It would do a terrible injustice to God's Word were we to allow this kind of thinking to be applied to it. We needed to make sure we understood how the Wilo people thought about such incidents so that we could know where possible misunderstandings were likely to occur. We needed to be able to not only speak the Wilo language, but to think like a Wilo person in order to communicate God's Word effectively to them.

Chapter 26

A Pretty Good Misunderstanding

I hadn't really wanted to spend the day rushing through the jungle, but, oh well...

I had planned on spending the day doing some office work. I wasn't feeling very energetic, so a sitting-down job suited me just fine. But before I settled into the day's routine, I went over to the house of Odowiya to visit for a little while and see what was going on in the village.

I found him sitting on his porch, getting ready to go somewhere. Our conversation went like this:

"Hi, Odowiya. How's it going?"

"Good. What are you doing, studying?"

"Yes, a bit. What about you?"

"I'm going upriver."

"Oh yeah? What for?"

"To get some paddles at Mapo's house."

At least that's how I understood the conversation to go.

"Who are you going with?" I asked.

"With Snail."

"Well, can I come?"

He smiled and said, "Sure."

I didn't really want to go, because I'm a homebody. But I knew it would be good for me. After all, what could it hurt? I mean, his boat wasn't very big, but with only the three of us we'd just blitz up to this guy's house, pick up the paddles, and come right back. An hour, max. I'd still have most of the day to get done all that needed to be done in my office. Right.

When I got to the boat I began suspecting that the day would not unfold at all like I had anticipated. I saw that not only was Snail going, but pretty much his entire household. Some of his neighbors were going, too. According to my quick calculations, by the time we all crammed into the canoe we were six kids, five women, three men, two babies, and two dogs.

Well, at least there was no sign of a partridge in a pear tree. But why would so many people want to go pick up a few paddles? It seemed a little odd.

The boat, heavy with humans, started laboriously up the river. My eyes kept being drawn to the sides of the canoe where all that separated us from the water's cold clutches was a miniscule amount of sideboard. I sat very still, and hoped that no fish jumped; the rippling effect might just be enough to swamp us.

As boat rides go, this one was mercifully uneventful, the only tense moment being when another boat passed us going the opposite direction. The resulting waves probably would have sunk us if I hadn't been desperately lifting up on the seat like I was.

We arrived safely at Mapo's house, but instead of entering and getting the paddles, we walked right past it and down a narrow path into the jungle. My suspicions were confirmed: this wasn't about paddles. And no, I wasn't likely to get much office study done today.

The following seven hours were spent walking uphill, downhill, and aroundhill over and over again. Occasionally we'd stop and the Wilos would climb up tall trees that for the most part resembled your average telephone pole. Only at the very top were there branches, and that's where the berries (not to be confused with paddles) were.

While the Wilos, old and young alike, frolicked in the high reaches of these trees, I amused myself with dodging the branches loaded with berries that they would snap off and drop down. This was when I learned the phrase for "Watch out!"

After getting the berries from one area, we'd be off and running to the next. For the most part I followed fast on the heels of Odowiya lest I get left in the dust, abandoned in the middle of the jungle.

He would tell me the names of the various trees as we went along and I'd attempt to write it all down, along with a brief description of the tree, while at the same time stepping over logs, ducking vines and branches, and picking spider webs and their corresponding spiders off my face.

Occasionally Odowiya would quiz me, asking me the name of some nondescript tree that he had pointed out to me earlier. When of course I wouldn't know the name, he would smile tolerantly and tell me again.

With the weary sun sinking toward the horizon, we finally made it back to the boat. We built a small fire and ate a bunch of berries. My feet were not amused with the abuse they had sustained over the past few hours, but no big deal; they're only feet.

"Just think," I said to myself while eating berries and picking remaining strands of a spider web out of my hair. "If I hadn't confused the word 'berries' for 'paddles', I would have missed out on this little adventure."

These musings seemed only to increase the pain in my feet, but overall I'd say it had been a pretty good misunderstanding.

Chapter 27

Twice Cursed

What happened when I judged a book by the cover

I'm ashamed to say that when I first saw Nanisa, I was almost overcome by an impulse to bolt into the nearby woods, much like the village children used to run from me when I first arrived. The only thing stopping me was my shallow sense of decorum. I was walking to the river for my evening bath, swatting at the swarms of gnats that followed me, and preoccupied with an annoying horsefly that buzzed around my ankles. When I looked up, she was just a few paces away.

I was startled, to say the least. In fact, I was somewhat repulsed, which, last time I checked, was not an ideal missionary sentiment. She was coming down the trail in the opposite direction, and there was no way to avoid her.

She was making her way slowly toward me, bent over at the waist to such an extent that, as she drew near, I found I was actually looking down at the back of her head. With each step she took, her face swayed back and forth mere inches above the grass and sand on the path.

She looked ridiculously old. Her long unkempt white hair hung down around her face. One arm was tucked under her while the other rested on her back, and her only apparel was a tattered skirt that hung from her emaciated body as an afterthought. A little boy walked a few paces in front of her, a string of fish in one hand, a machete half his size in the other.

The sight was all a little unnerving, but I was left with no option but to continue walking toward them. As we neared each other I hesitantly spoke a greeting.

At this point, I would not have been surprised had the old woman responded with a wicked cackle, uttering some unintelligible mutterings while pointing a gnarled, accusing finger at me. Instead, craning her neck upward, she peered at me without straightening. She smiled.

"Hi, Dah-wee. Are you going to take a bath?" she asked in a clear, friendly voice, with no hint of a cackle whatsoever.

"Yes, I am. Are you returning home?" I asked in reply, hoping my relief wasn't obvious. I was wishing I knew her name, because the typical Wilo greeting tended to include the person's name. She didn't seem to mind, though.

Nanisa chuckled and made an observation to the boy accompanying her, who then looked at me and chuckled too. I stepped aside to let them pass by on the narrow trail. As they continued on toward the village, Nanisa remained bent over as though carefully inspecting the ground she was walking on. I went on my way, embarrassed by my misguided initial reaction to her physical appearance.

Nanisa was one of the very few Wilos who lived with a substantial physical impediment. When seated in a hammock or on the ground, she looked like any of the other elderly village ladies. But when walking, she was different; she wasn't physically able to stand upright, and was forced to walk bent over at the waist at such an angle that her face almost scraped the ground.

The Wilos in the village claimed she was a victim of witchcraft. They told us that long ago, her refusal to marry a powerful witchdoctor had so enraged him that he cursed her with this deformity, assuring that she would be physically unappealing to any other man.

She did get married, however. In fact, she was one of two wives of the village grandpa who had almost killed one of his newborn twin granddaughters. Nanisa had been able to give birth to several children of her own, and in many other ways had carried out a normal existence.

But in a way, the Wilos were right: she was under a curse of sorts, a curse that encompasses all mankind and stretches back to Adam and Eve. Someone had died to release her from that curse, but she was oblivious; oblivious for now, but hopefully not for long.

Chapter 28

To ?B or Not to ?B

Join in dissecting the Wilo language. It's fun. Really...

To *?b* or not to *?b*; that was the question. In one of those curves that an unwritten language throws at you from time to time (actually, more like a knuckle-ball in this case), we found ourselves needing to come up with an answer. We were to discover that the answer was "It depends."

Assume, for one moment, that you have been tasked with developing an alphabet for a strange, newly discovered language called English. You want to isolate every single sound the language makes, and then determine which sounds will require their very own letter in the new alphabet.

Picture the initial process as that of running a language through a chopping block, severing each sound with a cleaver as it makes its appearance. One chop and you've isolated the *j* sound. Another chop and you've isolated the *n* sound, then the *r* sound, and you're well on your way. You hear the word cake, and you chop off the *k* sound. But then you realize that there are two different *k* sounds in that one word. The first one is said with a lot of breath behind it, while the other one employs virtually no breath at all.

What should you do? Should you swing the cleaver and separate the breathy *k* sound from the other *k* sound, or should you consider that they are the same consonant used twice in the same word, but pronounced differently? It would be poor procedure to just assume these two sounds are variations of the same consonant. They are technically two different sounds, so yes, you should indeed isolate them both.

During this initial step it is better to be too detailed than too general. In fact, it is impossible to be too detailed at this point. Your job, with the chopping block and cleaver, is to isolate every single sound you hear coming from the mouths and throats of those strange English speakers.

Once you're confident that you have isolated all the individual sounds of the language, your next step is to unite as many of the sounds as possible. Divide in order to unite.

Why would you try to unite sounds that you just got through isolating and separating? You do that because having a distinct alphabetical letter for every single sound in the language is unnecessary. Some of those sounds will not merit their own letter in the new alphabet.

You used the chopping block to perform the first step, now you need to get out the glue and unite a few of those sounds. So, how do you determine which sounds should get glued together? There is actually an entire science dedicated to this very thing. And believe me, it is not something that should be tried at home. Possible side-effects are dramatic hair loss, drowsiness, sudden outbreaks of hives, and irritability.

By reading the following paragraph, you are agreeing to not hold me liable for any injury or mental anguish that might result. Children under the age of fifteen should be accompanied by an adult, should they for some reason be reading this instead of playing video games or chatting on the internet.

To determine which sounds will need their own letter in the alphabet, and which sounds will just piggy-back on another sound, you have to analyze each sound in three different contexts. The first is the context of what the sound communicates. Does the sound carry with it grammatical significance, such as the *s* sound in English being used to pluralize nouns? The second is the context of the surrounding sounds that sandwich it. The third is the context of how the sound fits into the emerging distribution patterns of the language.

For instance, when analyzing the sounds of the Wilo language, we noticed that among many other sounds, we had a few sounds that had to pop out of the mouth, as opposed to easing out of the mouth. We called them pre-glottalized consonants. The *b* sound, the *d* sound, the *m* sound, and the *n* sound all had two different ways of being pronounced: either popping out of the mouth, or easing out of the mouth.

On the chopping block we separated all of them, and the pre-glottalized ones we wrote down as *ˀb*, *ˀd*, *ˀm*, and *ˀn*. Initially we thought these were four distinct and stand-alone sounds. But as we looked at them in the three different contexts mentioned above, we realized we could glue the *ˀm* to the *ˀb*, and the *ˀn* to the *ˀd*.

What did we notice that allowed us to make this determination? Thanks for your interest. What we noticed was that the *ˀb* sound and the *ˀd* sound occurred throughout the spectrum of the sound patterns of the language, *except for one particular environment*. They were never found in close proximity to any nasal sounds. That was suspicious. Why would these two sounds show up all over the place except around nasal environments? Were they prejudiced against nasal vowels and consonants?

And then we noticed that the *ˀm* sound and the *ˀn* sound showed up *only in company with other nasal sounds*. Lightbulbs went on. The *ˀm* sound, we concluded, was actually the *ˀb* sound just trying to fit into the nasal sounds around it – a kind of peer pressure, so to speak. It wasn't prejudiced at all. And the *ˀn* sound was in fact the *ˀd* sound employing the same sort of subterfuge. Though we had initially isolated the *ˀm* from the *ˀb* and the *ˀn* from the *ˀd* on the chopping block, we eventually determined that even though the *ˀm* and *ˀn* sounds did exist, there was no need for them to have their own letters of the alphabet. They were merely environmental variations of the *ˀb* and *ˀd*.

Hey! Wake up! It's your turn now. Remember how you had isolated two different variations of the k sound for English? One was breathy, and the other one wasn't. Should you keep them separate and give each one its own letter in the new alphabet?

If you were to follow the scientific guidelines and analyze each of those k sounds, you would discover that the breathy k shows up only at the beginning of words. Is that significant? Yes, it is, especially when you go a step further and realize that the breathless *k* is *never* found at the beginning of words.

Thus you, the scientist, would conclude that, since these two *k* sounds show up in their own mutually exclusive environments, you can indeed unite them and have them both be represented by a single symbol in the new alphabet.

So then, why isn't the word *cake* in English spelled *cace*, or *kake*? Well, I think the recess bell just rang. Class is over. We have answered the question, "To *ˀb*, or not to *ˀb*?" Your homework is to answer the question, "To *c*, or not to *c*?"

Chapter 29

Yeni

What a tribal girl can expect from life

"Where are you going?" the little girl asked in a voice so quiet I almost missed it. I had sat down a few feet away without paying much attention to her, so she must have determined it was up to her to get a dialogue started.

"I'm going upriver. Are you coming?" I knew she was, but thought I'd ask anyway.

Pleased that she had elicited a response from me, but not about to give me that same satisfaction, she answered with only a suddenly self-conscious smile.

Normally Yeni's day would consist of hanging around her mom; literally, in a carrying strap. Or sitting on the dirt floor of her house finding ways to entertain herself in the light the cooking fire provides, or keeping up with her siblings at play. Today was different. Today she was going on a boat ride.

It didn't take long for her family to gather together the things they needed for the trip. We all headed down to the river and soon were underway. A strong wind whipped the surface of the river into choppy waves, and as the dugout moved along, water began splashing into the boat, drenching everybody but those at either extreme. I mentally filed away this useful bit of information for future reference, since I was seated neither in the front nor the back and was suffering the chilly consequences.

I glanced over to where Yeni was sitting. Her little dress was soaked and beads of water ran down her face. She wasn't crying. Both hands clutched her mother's arm while she leaned her head against her mother's shoulder. Her eyes were shut tight and the corners of her mouth were pulled down into a little pout.

With each repeated spray that blew into the boat her body would stiffen and then relax. Occasionally she would press her face into her mother's shoulder as though silently imploring her to make it stop. At one point her eyes opened, and when she looked at me, I tried an isn't-this-fun smile, but whatever I was selling she wasn't buying and, rooted firmly in reality, her forlorn expression remained unchanged.

The wind eventually died down, and while the rest of the trip went smoothly, I was struck by how jungle hardships are accepted simply as facts of life by the Wilos, even by the very young.

If Yeni's life were to follow the pattern of a typical Wilo girl, she would spend the first few years of her life almost continually with her parents or siblings. One of her favorite pastimes would be to emulate her mother as she went about her daily responsibilities.

She might spend a few years attending a government-run school, where she would learn next to nothing because of the language barrier. She wouldn't go through a rebellious stage, but even as a child would be eager to incorporate herself into adult life. She'd get married in her teens to someone most likely of her own choosing and would possibly wind up sharing that position of wife with a second woman, although with the younger generation of Wilos that wasn't a common practice anymore.

She and her husband would both work hard to provide daily for their family. Yeni would have to get up early every morning to cut firewood, prepare a cooking fire, and begin her daily routine. They would work almost every day in their garden; they would haul heavy loads on their backs down long jungle trails. They would have to make a new house for themselves every five or six years because the jungle materials the Wilos used for their houses were susceptible to the ravages of termites and the elements. Like previous generations, Yeni's life would likely revolve around the tasks of day-to-day survival.

But there was something that might be different for Yeni. Sitting in the boat thinking about Yeni's future life, I felt hopeful that she, unlike those from generations gone by, would be able one day to have the opportunity to choose something other than the animism that was the default belief system of her people. This was a choice not previously available to those Wilos who had gone before. When she grew up, she would hopefully be able to decide whether to believe the Bible or to reject it. And that was exciting. None of her people had yet had that opportunity.

Chapter 30

A Perfectly Good Hunting Trip

An encounter with rodents, stingrays, and tarantulas

Shooting things has never been a passion of mine, but when a few of the Wilos invited me to go with them for a day of hunting, I figured it would be a great chance to spend some quality time out with the guys, a male bonding kind of thing. Glancing up at the sky, I saw nothing but beautiful blue. Maybe, just maybe, the torrential rains that generally dampen my adventurous spirit and my hunting trips would hold off.

"When are you going?" I asked them.

"Right now. Let's go," they replied urgently.

"I'll meet you at the boat," I said. Hurriedly gathering together a few pens and pencils and a notepad, I rushed down to the dugout. No one was there yet. I waited, and waited some more, swatting at the gnats that swarmed around my face and neck. Forty-five minutes later everybody joined me. We pushed the boat away from shore and headed upriver to where we would spend the day hunting.

The dugout eventually pulled into an area of jungle where the river was overflowing the bank. The hunting ground turned out to be completely flooded. I supposed we would have to continue looking for higher, drier ground, since scuba hunting had yet to become a Wilo pastime.

But no. Everybody was getting out of the boat and wading around in the chest-deep water. The idea, it soon became clear to me, was to spend the day pushing through the water, looking for the high places of ground where trapped animals might be taking refuge.

Everybody scattered, and I was left to frantically catch up to Odowiya and Snail. It's hard to frantically catch up to anybody when you're in water up to your chest, but desperate times call for manic measures, and I was up to the task.

I fell in behind them, and after sloshing around for a while we came across a hollow tree from which were emanating sounds that betrayed the presence of life. Either the resident termites were having a fiesta, or there was something resembling supper inside the tree.

For the next hour or so the hunters tried coaxing the animal out of its wooden bunker. They cut down a couple of long thin saplings and shoved them up into the hollow of the tree. They shook the tree; they struck it with poles and with their machetes. The goal, apparently, was to make life miserable for the poor shivering creature. Well, just because I was cold and miserable didn't mean I was a wimp. I could handle it. I had been miserable before; I was prepared to be miserable again. While the two Wilo men went about this business, I passed the time shivering and pretending I actually enjoyed spending hours flushing animals out of hollow trees while being stung by ants and mosquitoes and other assorted insects.

Finally a fifteen-pound rodent hesitantly stuck his head out of the tree. If his intent was to begin waving a white flag, he never quite got around to it, as he was promptly greeted by a sharp, pointed projectile.

Not satisfied with such a meager day's work, however, we continued slogging our way along. Occasionally the Wilos would notice stingrays in the murky water and would make wide detours. To me these stingrays didn't seem threatening. They looked like nothing more than delicious golden-brown pancakes gracefully gliding through the water, just waiting for someone to pour maple syrup on them, but that might be attributed to the fact that I had left my house without eating breakfast, since I had been told we were leaving "right now".

At one point, while Odowiya was climbing over a log, a red

hairy tarantula jumped up onto his leg. The quick-thinking Odowiya knew exactly what to do in this situation. He froze in mid-stride, turned around and, pointing at the tarantula crouched menacingly on his leg, said, "*Awuka*."

Learning cap firmly in place, I deduced that *awuka* was either an expletive or the name for the spider. Since repeating either one would likely be acceptable in this situation, I gave him a weak smile and tried to repeat the word back to him. After my third or fourth attempt he indicated he was satisfied with my pronunciation. Then he flicked the tarantula back onto the log and continued on, leaving me with the moral dilemma of choosing either to stomp the thing into oblivion or to gingerly step over it. I never have liked spiders much, anyway. Especially ones with a fondness for jumping onto passers-by.

A while later, as we were wading through knee-deep water, the two hunters in front of me shouted something unintelligible and jumped for the nearest trees. This was a little disconcerting, and as soon as my eyes had settled back into their respective sockets I determined that the wise course of action would be to follow their example. Thus persuaded, I grabbed a nearby branch and pulled myself up and out of the water, at the same time noticing two stingrays coming our way.

Considering this was the first time in my life to be treed by a stingray, I can hardly be blamed for choosing a tree that was a bit too small to effectively hold my weight. As I sensed the tree begin to slowly bend under me, I began lifting my feet to compensate for the distressingly rapid loss of clearance between me and the two stingrays that were quickly approaching.

None too soon, they passed underneath and I was able to unwrap my legs from around my ears. From then on I always took note of where the good climbing trees were.

Finally, soaked to the skin from slipping and sliding all day long, it was time to head for home. I pulled myself out of the water and into the boat. I glanced up at the storm clouds forming in the distance. "Ha!" I felt like shouting to the dark clouds. "You're too far away! This is one time you won't be able to soak me, and ruin a perfectly good hunting trip."

Chapter 31

The Wright Stuff

Missionary bush pilots are strange, but awesome

Way back in the olden days, missionaries to remote and isolated tribal locations had to be prepared to really rough it. For one thing, back then computers were not what we know them to be today. True, they had awe-inducing names like Whirlwind, Atlas, and Colossus, but they were unwieldy contraptions that filled entire rooms and as such, were not allowed as carry-ons on most airlines.

This did not deter the missionaries, however. Armed with determination, typewriters, and bottles of white-out, they went to some of the most rugged and inhospitable places on this earth, motivated by a desire to reach out to societies that few others cared about.

For these missionaries, traveling in and out of the tribal locations required days, sometimes weeks, of exhausting effort. Hours and hours of hiking through thick underbrush, days and days of river travel, shooting dangerous rapids, portaging around waterfalls, being bitten and stung along the way by ants, spiders, scorpions and other sundry jungle critters; that generation of missionaries had the right stuff.

I, on the other hand, had the Wright stuff. Those Wright brothers – bless them – must have had me in mind as they were tinkering in their workshops and taking flight in their dubious crafts. They were working on something that would make my life a lot easier, and I appreciate that, believe me.

As a result of their inquisitive endeavors, I didn't often have to hack my way through virgin jungle; that wasn't a hardship that fell to me. But that's not to say I lived life on easy street. Not at all. Sometimes I had to lean over and twiddle those annoying knobs on the communications radio for a long time when calling in a flight. On more than one occasion, when flying into the jungle, the airplane I was in got tossed about in a thundercloud, causing me to lose my place in the magazine I was reading, not to mention my lunch. And those seatbelts in the airplane! What were those things made of, anyway? Reinforced sandpaper? It was a lot to endure, but I tried not to complain, at least not within hearing of the missionary pilots who flew those airplanes.

They had to put up with quite a bit themselves. They were viewed by us jungle-bound missionaries as a Santa Claus of sorts, which is all fine and well, unless Santa doesn't bring gifts. Pity the pilot who should have the misfortune of landing at a remote missionary station without having thought to bring the mailbag.

I came to realize something about these missionary bush pilots: they see things that other people don't. I lost count of the times a pilot would land, dig out the mailbag and hand it over, wearily remove his helmet and then say something about there being a big dip in the middle of the airstrip. But no matter how many times I went out to look for myself, I never saw anyone there at all.

Poor guys. I think some of them were just overworked, that's all. What else would you expect from people who work from sunup to sundown flying across a sea of rugged jungle terrain? And flying was the easy part. The real work involved loading and unloading hundreds of pounds of cargo such as livestock, pets, food, combustible fuels, and household appliances. Their passengers ranged from children traveling to boarding school, crying as they left their parents, to government officials, to white-knuckled tribal people unfamiliar with air travel, to women in labor, to severe trauma victims, to corpses. Their reward for all of this was the opportunity to put their lives on the line by landing on short, narrow jungle airstrips with little wing clearance and big undulations in them, only to be greeted with a perfunctory: "Hi. Where's the mailbag?"

No doubt about it: these pilots, just like those old-time

missionaries, had the right stuff, whether they saw imaginary things or not.

Chapter 32

The Journal I Should Have Kept

A week spent fishing with the Wilos at the rapids

If I had owned a pith helmet I would have donned it as I jauntily stepped out the door and into a week of jungle adventure. Little else symbolizes the true explorer spirit like the pith helmet. However, a secondary symbol of the explorer is the journal. So, to prove my credentials as an explorer extraordinaire, I hereby present to you these daily entries of the journal that I should have kept while on this adventure.

Wednesday: *I bid farewell to my co-workers. I think nothing of their masterfully hidden tears, nor of their desperate but unvoiced pleas that I reconsider this dangerous excursion into the wilds. My mind is set; my heart has already gone before me. The unknown lies out there somewhere and how can I but move forward?*

I square my shoulders, swat at several obnoxious horseflies and, along with a group of friendly natives, embark upon this most phenomenal of fishing expeditions.

At noon, after several hours of sitting motionless in the dangerously overloaded canoe, we approach a tall clay riverbank upon which are constructed several primitive tribal dwellings. In the time-honored tradition of voracious vultures, we descend upon this unsuspecting village and eat all their food. Waddling back to the canoe an hour later, we provide big targets for any disgruntled hungry villager seeking revenge and left-overs, but we manage to leave unharmed and unhindered by all but our bloated stomachs. There is something to be said for at least half of this feast-or-famine mentality. With canoe even more overloaded, we continue upriver 'til darkness overtakes us. We pull up to sandbar, swing our hammocks and mosquito nets, and sleep under stars.

Thursday: Natives are restless and at dawn we break camp and continue journey. Several bends upriver, the navigator, standing tall in prow of canoe, notices turtle swimming under boat. His hands, as though connected to arms of rubber, instantly stretch down into water and snap rest of body after them. Surfaces empty-handed.

Late in the afternoon we finally arrive at rapids! ~~Herd Flock School~~ Bunch of monkeys protest our arrival by screaming and carrying on in the treetops. Tough. As we prepare shelter, torrential downpour drenches us. Fish soup for supper.

Friday: Awoke before dawn. Cooking fire was crackling, almost as loudly as my aching spine. Breakfast menu consisted of excessively ripe bananas smoked in the peel over the open fire. True explorers don't eat breakfast. Men fish all day long with little to show for it. Women not at all impressed. Tough. Fish soup for supper.

Saturday: Skip breakfast again. New fishing strategy revealed today. Instead of casting line into river, we must now swim out into raging torrent with baited hook in hand. Dive down 'til find bottom, insert hook upside down into riverbed and frantically swim back to dry ground before getting swept into the yawning mouth of hungry waterfall. One drawback to this new method is fish don't always wait for you to return to firm footing before taking the bait. Other drawback is finding riverbed with lip or forehead. Good catch today. Women properly impressed. Fish soup for supper.

Sunday: Pretty much same as Saturday. Wild turkey soup for supper. YES!

Monday: In the morning, men take leave of fishing duties and instead take to jungle foraging for fruit. On way back to camp, loaded down with stalks of palm fruit and guided by instincts of natural woodsman, I precede several natives down trail. Reaching especially overgrown section, I glance back to seek input on how to detour around obstacle. I see only an empty trail, but hear muted voices diminishing down a different trail. Could it be they would be so foolish as to question my directional instincts?

Unwilling to embarrass the natives by pointing out that they had taken the wrong trail, I scramble to fall silently into step behind them. I did not wish for them to get separated from me, as they would eventually be requiring my services when the trail petered out.

As luck would have it, they somehow stumble across the campsite anyway. We pack up our stuff, load up the boat with much smoked fish, and head downriver 'til darkness overtakes us. Sleep on sandbar under stars until midnight, at which point we sleep on sandbar under thunder-clouds and sheets of icy rain. Could really go for some of that fish soup right about now.

Tuesday: Home stretch. Only excitement when navigator knocked out of boat and into river by low-hanging tree branch. Other natives hide concern behind hysterical laughter. In effort to maintain atmosphere of light amusement, I later step out of boat pretending to be totally unaware of depth of water, which I find to be considerable. Natives seem pleased with this selfless gesture on my part. Perhaps they'll invite me on future expeditions.

Chapter 33

Hands to Yourself

Why do so many of the villagers want to get their hands on me?

I was sitting with several Wilos in the shade of a large tree that cast its shadow in the middle of the village, when I felt a sharp pain in my ankle, like someone had poked me with a sharp stick. With the pain came the realization: *Someone has just poked me with a sharp stick.*

Yes, it was that time of year again. It came with the rains. It was a time of year that tended to sneak up and take me unawares even though it showed up pretty much like clockwork every year, right around May or June. I should have seen it coming, but the fact of the matter is that there's not much I could have done to avoid it even had I been aware of its imminent arrival.

It was the time of year when the Wilos, generally a stoic people not much given to displays of emotion, were practically overcome by the desire to get their hands on me.

I should say right off that this was not my fault. I did nothing to bring this unwanted attention upon myself. I can tell you who the real culprits were: the gnats, that's who. Those tiny, black, blood-sucking flies were responsible.

During the summer months of rain, swarms of gnats prowled about in search of anything with a pulse. Once having detected a likely subject, they would then descend upon their victim with a gusto that bordered on the psychotic.

It was not uncommon for an hour of manual labor outside to be rewarded (if you can call it that) with thousands of gnat bites. The

115

only way to avoid this was to limit the amount of exposed flesh put at their disposal. This could be done by dressing up in long pants, long-sleeved shirt, and shoes, or else by applying several layers of greasy, smelly insect repellent. Since neither of these options was very appealing to me, the gnats, in turn, found me very appealing. Their enthusiasm knew no bounds as they bit into any exposed skin, and crawled into my ears, eyes, nose, and mouth.

Now, perhaps you're finding it difficult connecting all this information about the gnats to the fact that the Wilos longed to get their hands on me. Let me assure you that these two subjects are inextricably intertwined.

You see, when a gnat bites, he fills up on blood and then lumbers off, leaving in his wake a tiny weal topped by a speck of blood. This speck of blood subsequently dries and clings to the skin much like a minuscule scab. Fascinating, huh?

This is where the Wilos came in. They all seemed to possess a slightly pathological urge to pick these specks of dried blood off of each other. They'd pick up any twig at hand and proceed to dislodge the blood specks with a deft flick of the wrist.

I had yet to fully appreciate the therapeutic benefits derived from this practice, but the Wilos swore by it. Perhaps it is much the same as how certain people just can't leave a scab alone but have to be constantly picking at it, or how others can't resist popping those bubbles in packing material.

Gnat-bite picking, if done properly, is a procedure that is not painful in the least. It does, unfortunately, quite often result in little boil-like sores, particularly if the twig used in the procedure has had a less than sterile past, a condition common among village twigs that grow in areas where the bathroom is the great outdoors.

This was the time of year when the singing of birds and the pleasant background noise of wind rustling through the trees was drowned out by the ugly buzzing of gnats and the monotonous sound of hands slapping against flesh as everybody did what they could to defend themselves against the inexorable onslaught of these tiny marauders.

It was the time of year when everybody kept their hands waving about their face, and talked to each other through clouds of gnats. It was the time of year when the Wilos would gaze longingly at the many gnat bites dotting my legs and arms. They would raise their eyebrows approvingly and inform me that my gnat bites were just right to pick. They would whisper among themselves and the lust was almost palpable.

Occasionally a child would sneak up behind me while I was otherwise distracted and hurriedly pick at some of the specks before furtively retreating to study my reaction. The obsession was so great that I was often tempted to wear long pants instead of shorts, not to avoid being bitten by the gnats, but in order to hide the gnat bites from the Wilos. The attention and double-takes my blood-specked legs drew was enough to make any Marilyn Monroe envious.

Nevertheless, I was always happy when in December the swarms of gnats would, to a great extent, withdraw and regroup for the crusades of the coming year. Enough of being such a celebrity! For a few months I could go back to being just a normal pale-skinned person with no redeeming dermatological characteristics whatsoever.

Chapter 34

More Than Words

The importance of knowing what you're talking about

You wouldn't think it would be all that complicated. The phrase "It is over there" seems like a pretty straightforward statement. It's not confusing. It's not a complex sentence structure. I never realized how much that simple phrase could reveal about my language, and my world-view. I never imagined it would show me just what type of information is important to me, and what type of information I can do without, when communicating.

"It is over there." Not a very flowery phrase. It doesn't pack a lot of meaning, it doesn't stir a lot of emotion in us, unless of course, it is spoken in reference to an unclaimed winning lottery ticket or to an urgently needed bathroom. We just say it to let someone know where something is. No big deal. We point in a general direction and say it: "It is over there." It just means that the object, whatever it may be, is there, somewhere other than where we are.

For the Wilo people it is different. When they say, "It is over there", they want to know certain information about the *it* and the *is* and the *over* and the *there*. In fact, their language *requires* that a large amount of information be packed into this phrase.

A Wilo speaker, in order to say, "It is over there", would need to know and communicate certain peripheral information. Is the object living or non-living? Is the object in sight or out of sight? Is the object located on the ground? Is it resting on some other object? Is it suspended in the air? Is the object lying lengthwise like a ruler, standing upright like a can, or sitting like a ball?

You'd think that with the inclusion of all this information you would end up with a seemingly interminable, unwieldy sentence structure. That's how it would work in the English language. To include all that information, I would have to say something like, "The non-living thing is over there within sight, resting upright on something else."

Well, when a Wilo person says, "*Yai wa*", he is saying, "It is over there", but what the listener can glean from that short phrase is that the non-living thing which is in sight is resting over there on something else. When he says, "*Yai olobe*", he is again saying, "It is over there", but this time he is communicating that the living thing is over there out of sight, suspended in the air. It is impossible to say "It is over there" without specifying all of these things.

A common misconception among many people in the world is that primitive cultures have simplistic, underdeveloped languages. I can tell you from personal experience, it just ain't so. Perhaps closer to the truth is the statement that the more primitive the people group, the more complex the grammar of their language. It is not surprising that tribal languages have been used as military code for armies in the past.

We found the Wilo language to be terribly complex as we initially struggled to understand it and decipher its meanings. Over time, however, it changed to being *wonderfully* complex to us as the pieces began to fall into place. It was like putting together an enormous jigsaw puzzle. Now if only we had the picture on the box to guide us in the process!

Chapter 35

DNA Gone Bad

There may be genetic culpability for my struggles in learning the Wilo language

I don't doubt the Wilos thought I was a little dense. Not only had I fallen short of their expectations, but I had succeeded in smashing those naive expectations into so many little pieces.

Initially they thought I'd learn their language in a few short months. After those few months had gone by and they could see I was still having trouble saying even the simplest of things, they adjusted their expectations and gave me a full year. Thanks, guys. That's real generous.

And then, when several years had come and gone and I was still valiantly struggling *mano a mano* with their language, they would smile tolerantly and say, a bit wistfully and not too optimistically, "Someday soon."

And then one day, it happened. No, I didn't suddenly learn the language. But I did have an epiphany of sorts, a glorious moment of self-discovery. I came across some information that caused me to realize that this prolonged learning curve wasn't necessarily my fault; that perhaps there was medical culpability of the genetic kind. What great news! Let me explain.

Every language has its own grammatical patterns. Languages such as English use what is mostly a word-based grammar system, a system where grammar is structured primarily on the order of words. When we say, "The branch fell and hit Brian," we picture Brian walking under a tree when all of the sudden, a branch cracks and falls on him. Ouch.

If we use those same words, but put them in a different order, we come up with a totally different scenario: "Brian fell and hit the branch." Now what we might picture is Brian climbing high in a tree, losing his grip and falling, striking a branch on the way down. Ouch. Same words, same hospital trip for Brian, but a completely different scenario because the sequence of the words was switched around. That's how English works.

There are other languages, though, that go about things differently. These languages rely more on suffixes, prefixes, and infixes to construct thoughts and sentences. With these kinds of languages, a single word might contain a subject, a verb, an object, a verb tense, and various other grammatical features.

The Wilo language is definitely geared toward suffixes and prefixes. When I say, "*Wiwiekwahabetho ubudekwabito*", what I'm saying with those two words is, "After he accidentally repeatedly got cut, he cried today for a long time." Thirteen words in English are condensed into two words in Wilo.

Yet it isn't as easy as learning all the various suffixes and prefixes and simply tacking them onto the central word haphazardly. You need to know which ones can be used in conjunction with others, what the sequence should be, and what your focus, as a speaker, should be on.

"So, Davey," you might be wondering by now, "what exactly is your point? What does this have to do with genetics? Will you next be telling us what the price of tea in China is?"

No, I shan't. But I'll tell you why I may not have been at fault in taking so many years to learn the Wilo language. I happened upon an article in a reputable magazine claiming that researchers have discovered a certain gene mutation that shows up as an inability to correctly put suffixes onto words. Lyserious! Um... I mean "Seriously!" For an English speaker, this type of genetic malfunction is bad enough; for a Wilo it would spell disaster. The poor genetically mutated individual would be incapable of saying practically anything. Which is exactly the situation I found myself in when starting out learning the Wilo language.

So, there you have it. This no doubt explains the delay in my gaining fluency. I should have gotten tested. Perhaps my language gene was only partially mutated, which would explain how I seemed to experience little difficulty using suffixes in the English language.

A positive test result would have proven that it's all my DNA's fault, thus lifting a heavy load of poor self-esteem off my weary shoulders. Perhaps it could have even been considered my parents' fault, which seems to be the socially correct place to deposit unclaimed blame these days.

It certainly made me feel better knowing I was free of blame. I would have put down the magazine and rushed out to explain this wonderful news to the Wilos, but I knew I wouldn't be able to without using a mountain of suffixes. The fact that it wasn't my fault would have to be my little secret.

Chapter 36

No Therapy Required

What happens when a tribal boy is given away

Have you ever had one of those special moments when, *apropos* of nothing much, you ask yourself where culture ends and the universal laws of nature begin?

Of course you have! Only the most socially irresponsible among us would have failed to grapple with such a momentous question. I myself spent several long seconds wrestling with this very issue and wound up concluding that I had just been pinned to the mat. It was a slippery question indeed, hard to get a grip on.

For instance, it is cultural that some people in this world sleep on mats on the floor. Others sleep on beds, others in hammocks, depending on the culture. The universal law, though, is that people from every culture require sleep. Certain things are specific to a culture, while other things are universal.

In Pakali, a young married woman named Woodpecker gave birth to a baby boy. She didn't go to a hospital to give birth. She didn't hire a midwife to help in the process. She didn't have an epidural, or any other drug. She was a hundred miles from the nearest town, so she gave birth in the same way her people had been doing for generations: outside in the dirt, with little fanfare and ceremony. When the baby was born, the umbilical cord was cut using the serrated edge of a pineapple leaf.

The newborn baby was not given a Wilo name initially; that would come at a later point when the child's antics brought inspiration. But well before we missionaries showed up on the scene, many of the Wilos had been giving their newborn children

Spanish names, and this baby was no exception; he was named Osnerol.

Osnerol was a typical Wilo baby. He spent the majority of his time in someone's arms or perched in a carrying strap. He never learned to crawl all that well because he spent so little time on the ground. He didn't go through a baby-talk phase, because his parents and other adults didn't talk to him much in baby talk.

As a result, it seemed as though he wasn't developing at a proper pace. He wouldn't speak (at least not when I was around), and I never witnessed him learning to stand or totter about on his feet. So it came as quite a shock when, one day, I realized he had somehow mastered both speaking and walking. Where had that come from? He was running around with his older siblings, and speaking in full sentences.

And then his mom gave him away. She had a relative who had not been able to have any children, and since she already had two children of her own, she gave Osnerol to her barren sister. Everyone agreed that was very thoughtful of her.

And that's when I entered into the wrestling ring to grapple with that philosophical question of culture versus universal law. "Where," I wondered, "is all the emotional trauma that would naturally flow from such an arrangement? What about the yearnings the birth mother would feel when she sees her child going to the garden with that other family? Wouldn't it devastate her to see her son Osnerol bonding with his new family? After all, they live only a few houses apart. Wouldn't her maternal instincts make her want to reach out and take her child back? Surely the turmoil of emotions brought about by seeing her child grow up in the home of another would leave her an emotional wreck.

"And what of the child?" my pondering continued. "Wouldn't Osnerol cry at night because he misses being with his first family? Would he grow up feeling rejected and unwanted? Would he hate his birth parents? Would he be a maladjusted adult later in life? Wouldn't he suffer from low self-esteem?

"Surely being given away in such a seemingly cavalier manner would be bound to create inner turmoil in the life of the child, right? Isn't there a universal law dictating that being given away as a child be classified as a hardship, or at the very least a stigma of some kind? Wouldn't that be an emotional blow in any culture?"

Having wrestled thus with these questions and so having fulfilled my social responsibilities, I left it to Osnerol and the others involved to speak for themselves. The transition from one family to another seemed to be a perfectly natural thing. It raised no eyebrows in the community, it created no *angst*, and all parties involved, including Osnerol, simply adjusted to their new status and continued on with their lives. The new parents were happy, the old parents were happy, the child was happy. No therapy required.

Chapter 37

Propriety of Speech

Why did God have to create grammar?!

My dictionary defines grammar as: "A system of principles and rules for speaking or writing a language; propriety of speech."

Propriety of speech? If pressed to give my own definition, it would tend to include a certain degree of *im*propriety of speech.

OK, maybe that's an overstatement. Grammar is like an incorrigible child: better to be understood than disparaged, no matter how tempting the latter might be. I maintain, however, that unlike the incorrigible child, grammar should be heard, not seen. But enough about my childhood.

I mention this not because of my burning hatred of all things grammatical, but because a good chunk of our language study time in the village was taken up with the pursuit of dissecting the Wilo grammar down to its most minute details. Word order, suffixes, prefixes, infixes, postfixes, a-fixes, and quick fixes all were broken down into their smallest meaningful components which were then analyzed as to how they seemed to clarify or qualify or quantify the overall idea being communicated.

Grammar lovers (a strange breed of people unto themselves) have at times described such endeavor in glowing terms such as "a natural high" and "dreamy", which, although short on originality and sounding a bit like Woodstock, does go a long way in explaining that floating sensation and extreme drowsiness I would often experience near the end of our grammar sessions.

Our missionary team would get together and brainstorm grammar issues from time to time. Our discussions would go something like this:

Phyllis: "… So that's why it seems to me the suffix *eba* – well, actually just the letter *b* in the suffix – is used to indicate a transient aspect of the predication. The letter *a* maybe marks predication specifically. The letter *e*? I'm not too sure. What do you think, Tim?"

Tim: "I'd say the letter *e* indicates the initiation or commencement of that transient action. It's there to let you know a change has taken place, whether it be a new action or a new state of being. I don't know… How does that sound to you, Davey?"

Davey: "Huh?"

Tim: "What do you think about the focus being on the initiation aspect of the verb?"

Davey: "Ummm, well, yeah. I think it's a definite possibility."

Phyllis, chuckling: "A definite possibility? Isn't that an oxymoron?"

I was hurt, and retorted: "Of course it's an oxy, you doofus! Now, can we please stop calling each other names and just focus on the task at hand?"

OK, maybe that's an overstatement. We did actually make progress during these sessions, which is a good thing, because the Wilos themselves were at a loss to explain their grammar to us in any detail. Their answer to our dilemma was, "Hey, don't ask us. When you learn to speak well, you can explain to us why we say it like that."

Our only recourse was to pull out fistfuls of hair in frustration (although we were careful to limit this to our own hair) and then continue accumulating tons of language data, looking for patterns that would unlock to us the secrets of the structure of the Wilo language.

And you know, I started to really enjoy that grammar stuff. Who knew I could plumb such depths of joy spending hours on end charting the wonderfully capricious meanderings of the Wilo grammar? Our brainstorming sessions seemed to never be long enough, and believe it or not, I actually began to enjoy leisurely leafing through grammar reference books in my spare time. The unthinkable was beginning to happen: I was falling in love with grammar.

Yeah, you're right; that's an overstatement, too.

Chapter 38

The Wilo Family Tree

It's important to know you're not marrying family

There are many pastimes I would choose to pursue before taking up genealogy: pastimes such as chewing tin foil, and pouring jalapeño juice into my eyes. No, I have never attempted to chart out my family tree. But if I were ever to do so, my family tree would look much different than a corresponding family tree of a Wilo person.

Take, for instance, brothers and sisters. What do I call any sibling of mine who happens to be of the male gender? Well, depending on how we're getting along at the time, I might call him any number of things. But if I were charting out a family tree, I would call such a person my brother.

Likewise, any female sibling I have, I would put down as my sister. No problem. That's about as straightforward and unambiguous as you can get. After all, everybody knows that to be a brother or a sister you have to have the same parents. Why, even the dictionary confirms that to be a sibling there must be at least one parent in common. It's a universal truth, spanning continents and cultures. It's something we all view the same. I mean, how could it be otherwise?

Well actually, no. It isn't as universal as I might have assumed. It can indeed be otherwise. Sometimes brothers aren't necessarily brothers, nor are sisters always sisters. Sometimes relations are relative to the culture you live in.

I don't mean to imply that the Wilos don't have brothers or sisters. They do. Like ourselves, the Wilos have people whom they consider to be brothers and sisters. In fact, the Wilos tend to have a whole slew of brothers and sisters. This is how it works: if I were a Wilo, anybody with the same mother and father as me would automatically be considered either my brother or my sister. So far so good. That fits the pattern I'm used to.

But this next bit is where it gets tricky. As a Wilo, I would have several fathers and mothers. My biological father's brothers would all be considered my fathers, and the sisters of my biological mother would all be considered my mothers. The significance of this is that all the children of my father's brothers would be my brothers and sisters, since their dad is also my dad. Also, the children of my mother's sisters would be considered my brothers and sisters, since their mom is also my mom. That's kind of odd. My cousins are my brothers and sisters?

The answer to that is: yes and no, because while the children of my father's brothers and the children of my mother's sisters are my siblings, the children of my father's sisters and the children of my mother's brothers are no relation to me at all. And not only are they no relation to me; they form the ideal pool from which I might choose a marriage partner for myself.

So, while some of my cousins are considered siblings, others are considered prime marriage material.

Did you follow that? I'd repeat it all, but the easier thing would be for you to simply move your eyes up a few paragraphs and reread it.

So, what all of this makes me wonder now is: what was the relationship between Mary the mother of Jesus, and Elizabeth the mother of John the Baptist? The Bible, in Luke 1:36, states that they were kinfolk, or cousins. But looking at their kinship through the perspective of the Wilo culture, they might be considered sisters. That, in turn, would make Jesus and John the Baptist brothers. Hmmm...

Obviously, the family connection between Mary and Elizabeth is not of great consequence, as far as the gospel message goes. It is, though, a simple example of how clear and effective communication requires an understanding of the culture of the listener. Looking at their relationship through the grid of the Wilos, were Mary and Elizabeth sisters, or were they no relation at all? Does the Bible even give enough information to conclude one way or the other?

For our missionary team, learning about the kinship system of the Wilos was not only a way to better understand many aspects of their culture, but was also necessary for a clear presentation of God's Word. After all, many accounts of the Bible revolve around family relationships.

Chapter 39

Greener Than Thou

The plight of the palm-tree grub spurs me to environmentalism

I didn't leave civilization and go to the jungle with the purpose of getting involved in environmental protection. I'm not a tree hugger, although on occasion I have, out of necessity, hugged one or two, usually in order to escape the clutches of an animal that I desperately hoped wasn't an experienced tree hugger itself.

However, spending time with the Wilos in their own environment did have the unexpected result of making me become more concerned with the preservation of certain aspects of the Amazon jungle. Things that I witnessed and experienced among them caused me to be "greener" than I might normally have become, usually around the gills.

One such instance was when I found myself in the house of Buchi. I happened to poke my head into his doorway right around supper time. He invited me in and before I knew it, I was holding in my hand one of the cutest little jungle creatures you could imagine.

Looking down and gazing upon this tiny integral piece of the fabric of the Amazon jungle caused me to suddenly become uncharacteristically contemplative. I wondered: have any studies been conducted to determine if the Amazon palm-tree grub belongs on the endangered species list?

This little guy resting in my hand was really quite adorable: white as a lamb, with a head that looked like a shiny little black button. He was about the size of a big toe, and with similar culinary appeal. The more I looked at this cute little fellow, the greener I got.

I suddenly found myself burdened by the plight of this grub and others of his kind. Not many people care about underprivileged larvae; few people appreciate their uniqueness and inimitable qualities. In fact, the Wilo people, with total disregard for any environmental havoc they may be wreaking in the process, often chopped down perfectly good palm trees and enticed large populations of innocent and gullible grubs to form colonies in the rotting wood, only to later gleefully harvest these same grubs and dispatch them in what can only be described as a revolting and nauseating manner.

To make matters worse, they were known to offer up these poor creatures to missionaries, encouraging them to be complicit in this environmental travesty. They would excitedly proffer a handful of them and insist that the missionary eat them in order to learn to speak more fluently.

Well, I thought, enough is enough. Don't these people care even just one iota about their environment? Don't they understand that with the harvesting of these grubs they may unwittingly be depleting a lifeform upon which the existence of the entire jungle hinges?

This was not acceptable. I determined that these grubs needed an advocate. They needed someone who would take their side, someone who would object strenuously to the harassment of their peaceable colonies. If no such advocate was to be found, perhaps I'd have to take up that mission of mercy myself in my spare time.

I was of the conviction that these grubs be allowed to live and flourish and become whatever they wanted to become, sovereign and unopposed in their pursuit of the good life. I believed that, even in death, they should remain undisturbed and protected from the cruel grasp of those who would not only eat them, but also encourage and even expect others to do likewise.

This, in my humble opinion, would be a noble cause. The personal economic benefits would be negligible, of course, since one must assume that grub advocacy be done *pro bono*. Taking up the cause of these grubs would not be a career builder by any means. But it would be payment enough just to get the grubs off the dinner table. Success would be its own reward.

Chapter 40

Pulling a Joseph Crater

What do the Wilo people think when someone mysteriously goes missing?

Considering the dangers lurking in the river, along the riverbanks, and throughout the jungle, you might assume that the Amazon jungle is a very dangerous place to hang out, indeed. With alligators, anacondas, piranhas, jaguars and such skulking about, surely Wilo people often fall prey to such dangers.

But no. It is actually quite rare to come across an aggressive, man-hungry animal anywhere in the jungle. More often than not, people in the jungle are hurt by animals when they stop paying attention to their surroundings. Drop your guard, maybe get distracted by a beautiful butterfly or a pesky fly, and you might inadvertently stumble across a protective parent or offend a territorial, ill-tempered beast by, for instance, stepping on it or trampling its home.

So the Wilos have learned to be observant as they walk through the jungle and travel along the river. It's extremely rare for a Wilo person to go off on their own and never come back. It's not common, but it does occasionally happen. Once in a while someone just mysteriously disappears. It happens the world over. One minute the person is there, the next thing you know, they're gone. In many cases the missing person's fate remains an unsolved mystery.

When this happens among the Wilos, more often than not the missing person is last seen near the river. They go to the river perhaps to fish or to bathe, and they are never seen again. And while a good number of possible scenarios might come to our minds as to what could have happened to them, as far as the Wilos are concerned, there is but one probable explanation: they get kidnapped; kidnapped by roving evil spirits.

Although subsequent searches are made, they're rather perfunctory. The searchers might look along the banks of the river for a short distance, or do a cursory search through the trees looking for hints of what might have happened, but the truth is that they hold out little hope of ever seeing the missing person again. They resign themselves to accepting the cards the spirits have dealt them.

At the same time, they're careful to not say anything disrespectful of the spirits. Should they offend an eavesdropping spirit by criticizing or speaking harshly about them, the "kidnapped" person might be killed out of hand and left on a jungle trail somewhere. So when the Wilos hear of someone just out of the blue disappearing, they simply and quickly attribute it to the evil intervention of the spirits.

That being the case, what would the typical Wilo think when hearing for the first time the biblical accounts of both Enoch, and Elijah? The Bible tells us that Enoch didn't die, but just disappeared and "was no more". And Elijah was taken up to heaven in a supernatural chariot that came for him. Very mysterious circumstances, these.

How would the Wilos interpret such mysterious disappearances? Even though the Bible makes it clear that it was God who took up these two individuals, would they overlook that explanation and attribute it instead to the evil spirits?

Maybe they would conclude that they had been wrong about what happens to people who disappear; maybe they would change their minds and begin believing that it is actually God who kidnaps missing people, and not the evil spirits, as they had believed.

As we progressed in our study of the Wilo language, we were better able to investigate these areas of cultural beliefs because we were finally getting to the point where we could not only ask questions, but actually understand the answers and explanations the Wilos gave.

We are all possessed of a cultural grid, and it is this grid that guides us to make assumptions, draw conclusions, and arrive at our own particular understanding of the world around us, as well as of the afterlife. New information tends to get filtered through our cultural perspective without us even being aware of it. A clear and effective communicator will insist on understanding the cultural perspective of the listener.

Even when communicating with close friends and family who share our own cultural grid, we at times fail to communicate clearly. In a cross-cultural setting, miscommunication is a certainty, unless great care is taken to understand how any new information will be interpreted. To clearly teach the Bible message, we would need to do more than simply talk like the Wilos; we would need to think according to their cultural perspective. It wouldn't be sufficient to deliver the gospel message only to their ears; we must be prepared to navigate that message through their existing perspective, and accompany it until it is delivered intact, safe and sound, directly to their understanding.

For example, early on in the book of Genesis we find that God caused a deep sleep to fall upon Adam, and then, while Adam slept, God removed a part of his flesh and with it he formed Eve.

The Wilos believe that very powerful witchdoctors have the ability to cause their enemies to fall into profound sleep. While his enemies are sleeping, the witchdoctor can then kidnap their children, molest their women, and do any other harm that comes to his mind.

The Wilo perspective then, is that the act of putting someone into a deep sleep is an act of hostility and aggression. It is something an angry witchdoctor might do to his enemy.

Was that the context in which God put Adam into a deep sleep? If we spoke this account only to their ears, the Wilos might conclude that God is a powerful witchdoctor; that God was angry with Adam, and in his anger he formed Eve.

Verbal communication doesn't exist in a vacuum. The power of words lies not in the speaking of them but in the mental association the listener applies. Our goal as missionaries was to not only pronounce the truths of the Bible, but to proclaim them clearly and unambiguously. Sometimes though, I wondered if we would ever get to that point.

Chapter 41

Lifeforma Non Grata

The do's and don'ts of sharing your house with other life forms

The occasional visitor to my house in the village was likely to be surprised to find that I shared my residence with certain other life forms. It was a big house, with plenty of room, so why not? I tried to be hospitable that way.

But I was careful to not let just any ol' body set up house. It wasn't on a first-come-first-served basis. No, sirreee. I was selective. In spite of the societal pressure to be politically correct, I discriminated in regard to whom I allowed the opportunity to share my space. This discrimination was based primarily on appearance and lifestyle.

Perhaps that was crass of me, insensitive and all that. But well, it was my house, thank you very much. Besides, as I have mentioned, I was not indiscriminate in my discrimination. Not at all. I employed a very practical and completely objective standard to underpin my discriminatory policies. I used something that was established long, long ago: namely the food-chain principles.

In my estimation, it is incumbent upon everybody to give close attention to food-chain principles. I'm not referring to food chains such as MacDonald's or Wendy's, although those food chains should always be on the radar as well. The food chain I am referring to is the one that relates to the hierarchy of the animal kingdom, namely who eats whom, and who inflicts harm upon whom.

I found that taking these two issues into account helped me

avoid unnecessary pain and hardship. Furthermore, when combined with measurements taken using the grossness scale, these food-chain principles provided an effective guide to life forms with which one can successfully co-habit.

Take the cockroach, for instance. Take it very far away. Could there be a lower, more disgusting life form on earth? I think not. All they ever did all day was nibble my food on the sly and commit hygienic indiscretions randomly and prolifically throughout the house.

When I evaluated their resident status based on the food-chain principles, I asked myself, "Would I be in danger of being consumed by a cockroach?"

No. That was a point in favor of the cockroaches. Then I asked, "Would a cockroach inflict harm upon me?"

Again the answer was, no. That was another point in their favor. Unfortunately for the cockroaches, there remained one more daunting test. How would they measure on the grossness scale? Would they score low enough – it's a good thing to score low on this particular test – to qualify for co-habitation privileges?

When I tabulated their test results, I found that their scores on the grossness scale were through the roof. What this meant was that the cockroaches necessarily fell victim to the grossness rule. In spite of their benign status on the food chain, they were definitely *lifeforma non grata*.

Next to be evaluated were the spiders. If the spiders in question had the disturbing physical appearance of being on steroids – big, husky, and aggressive – they definitely got the boot, or the sandal, depending on which happened to be closer to hand. Although these spiders wouldn't eat me, they would likely inflict harm upon me, given half a reason and a reasonable chance.

On the other hand, the skinny brown spiders, those with the long gangly legs, were proffered shelter and the opportunity to unobtrusively weave their webs and hang around inside. After all, not only were they harmless to me, but they were also willing to earn their keep by eating insects that illegally immigrated into the house.

If there were an animal to rival the cockroach in grossness, it would have to be the bat. Most of the bats that attempted to hang out in my house were of the relatively harmless type, but I didn't want any of their evil-intentioned, blood-sucking relatives to be sneaking in under the radar, so to speak. For that reason, all bats were declared *lifeforma non grata*. Besides, how many other life forms have convinced us humans to come up with a special name for their own specific, well, guano? Not too many. I think that's concession enough for them.

Then there were the little lizards. Not only were they willing to hunt down and eat all sorts of *lifeforma non grata*, they were even considerate enough to occasionally change their colors in order to unobtrusively blend into their surroundings, thus maintaining a pleasantly low profile. They were allowed to stay, as long as they were discreet and stayed out of the way.

Anything that was higher than the lizard on the food chain, such as rats and possums and other things that go bump in the night, were not welcome in my house, regardless of the number of cockroaches they might be willing to consume in order to earn their keep. And anything that was equal to or higher than me in the food chain was the ultimate *lifeforma non grata*. If any such character were to show up in my house, I would act swiftly and decisively. They'd have to eat my dust before sinking their teeth into me.

Chapter 42

The Interrogation of a Suffix

The day I got medieval on a suffix

Let's get something straight. I've had to deal with my fair share of tough suffixes, and frankly, they make me sick. They give you the big run-around, they act like you don't know nothin'. When you get tough with them, they clam right up. That's right. Wringing a confession out of a reluctant suffix is like coaxing sunshine from an angry cloud.

So forgive me if I didn't exactly tap dance across cloud nine when my pleasant, tranquil day was shattered by one of these jokers showing up. Suffixes can be tough to break, and I could see that this one was going to be no exception.

I had brought him in, and he was nonchalantly sitting on the corner of my desk, on top of some other papers that were strewn across the weathered old surface. With my pen clenched between my teeth, I leaned back in my chair and glared at him for several minutes, thinking just maybe he would start sweating if I were to give him the silent treatment.

I don't like strange suffixes showing up. As far as I'm concerned they're delinquents, real lowlifes, if you know what I mean. I had found this one hanging out with a respectable verb in a nice residential area. I was shocked, let me tell you. I knew that verb! He went to *church*, for cryin' out loud! What was he doing rubbing shoulders with this... with this... this scum of a suffix?

Now, I ain't prejudiced against suffixes. Let me be clear on that. I get along real well with most of them. But until you get to know them, until you get to understand what makes them tick, they're just a real pain, if you get my drift. They go around with this superior smirk on their face, and it just basically gets on my nerves, know what I mean? It's not like the world revolves around them. It's not like they can make up their own rules. But this one was trying to be cute, so I hauled him down to the precinct.

When I gave him the silent glare, he was real cool, let me tell you. He just sat there on my desk, pickin' his teeth and lookin' up at the ceiling with that inscrutable smirk that says volumes.

"I don't remember seeing you around these parts before," I finally said.

"So?" he shrugged. "Ever thought maybe you should pay more attention? If you did, I think you'd recognize this pretty little mug." With that he framed his ugly face with his hands.

I slammed my fist down on the desk and he jumped. "So maybe you should just crawl back under whatever rock it was you crawled out from," I snarled. "We don't need your kind around here making trouble and infecting everybody with your... with your, uh... subtle influences."

I rummaged around on my desk and exhumed a black binder. "Let's just see if we have any kind of rap sheet on you," I smiled. It wasn't a pleasant smile.

He sat quietly while I flipped through the pages. Nothing. Go figure. I gave him a long hard look and he started squirming. He wasn't stupid. He knew the drill.

"You're not makin' this easy, pal, you know that," I said. "Believe me when I say this is gonna hurt me more than it does you." With that, I proceeded to take him apart piece by piece. It wasn't much fun – for either of us – and it probably violated some kind of suffix rights, but I was beyond caring. As hour faded into hour, I searched for clues as to his identity. I took the pieces down to forensics, I put them under a microscope, I ran some computer analysis, I called the other precincts; the works. I did everything short of what I really wanted to do, namely an autopsy. Still, I drew a blank. It just didn't make sense.

I took him back to the neighborhood where I had found him. When people passed by I asked them if they recognized this suffix.

Everybody said no. I couldn't believe it! It was lookin' like I was gonna have to let this clown go because of lack of evidence.

On a hunch, I grabbed a nearby verb and put the two together. Bingo! Now everybody was saying they knew who he was. They said they'd seen him carousing with other verbs, too. Apparently this turkey really got around, but nobody could actually pin down what he did for a living. All they could give me was circumstantial evidence. It was no good.

"Thanks. Thanks for nothin'," I growled to no one in particular. I took down the names of the other verbs he had been seen with. That'd give me a place to start, anyway. Maybe something would turn up.

For now though, I had no choice but to let the suffix go. "I hear Addis Ababa is real pretty this time of year," I said pointedly. "But around here you better watch your step, 'cuz if I spot you hanging out with another verb, I'll bring you in again. Don't think I won't. You hear what I'm sayin'?"

He left. Oh, he was scared, all right. I could tell by his inscrutable smirk.

Chapter 43

No Pain, No Gain

Those things embedded in my feet – are they thorns, or acupuncture needles?

The invitation in and of itself wasn't harmful nor in any way prejudicial to my well-being, but when combined with my foolhardy acceptance it took on a quality of sinister foreboding.

One of the guys in the village had recently made a fish spear for me: a length of bamboo, a metal point, and a band of rubber attached to the end. So when invited to join a boatload of guys for a fun day of diving into the water to spear fish, how could I refuse?

"Spearing fish? Why yes. I'd love to go," I said. It seemed the majority of my outings with the Wilos ended with some sort of physical or emotional discomfort, if not outright trauma, being inflicted upon me. But like a child to a hot stove, I was drawn to this opportunity to spend the day spearing fish with the Wilos. Besides, this might just be that perfect day-trip I had been waiting for. I envisioned myself, the intrepid fish spearer, doing some serious damage to the fish population. At the end of the day I was to be disappointed only in that most of the damage I wrought turned out to be self-inflicted. But I'm getting ahead of myself.

Propelled by an outboard motor of dubious integrity, our dugout canoe wound its way up the Balawa River. We eventually approached the shore, and pushed and pulled our way through some branches and up into a small tributary. We carefully maneuvered around logjams, boulders and sandbars until we came to a section of jungle where the river had flooded its banks, creating a large lagoon with surprisingly clear water. The plan for the day was to hang out under the surface of the water and spear unsuspecting fish as they swam past.

The fish, perverse in nature as usual, were not nearly as unsuspecting as I might have wished, and they refused to hang out in any area other than where there were dangerous logjams and razor grass galore. Not only that, but, much to my chagrin I seemed to be experiencing technical difficulties in mastering the finer points of spearing fish with the necessary amount of stealth and subtlety. How does one remain submerged under water while both hands hold the spear, poised to shoot?

I would dive down to the riverbed, holding the spear at the ready. So far so good. Fish would swim by tantalizingly close, but slowly, relentlessly my buoyancy would take over and I would feel myself being taken up to the surface. The fish would watch and snicker as I floated helplessly out of range before I could get off a shot.

I tried to surreptitiously stay down by flapping my ears and flexing my toes, but to no avail. The Wilos told me later that with flexing my toes I had been close to discovering the secret of staying submerged; they grab on to small roots or weeds with their toes and are thus able to remain anchored underwater while using both hands to work the spear.

In spite of the technical challenges, however, I soon had speared my retrospectively established quota of one fish, although I continued to swim around pretending to flail futilely at the other few that passed by.

As the day neared a close, with sunburned skin and assorted cuts and scratches on my legs, I decided I'd head for the boat and wait for the rest of the guys there. Ducking under the water and kicking out strongly, my foot was brought up short by a submerged palm tree, one that boasted thousands of inch-long thorns, although my foot had just relieved it of a dozen or so in one fell swoop.

The sensation was not so much that of acupuncture as *acute* puncture, and I was immediately impressed with the need to

146

express my feelings in an open and honest manner. But I refrained, not wanting the other swimmers to assume an alligator had me in its clutches. Instead, I continued on to the boat and busied myself with extracting the little dears.

When the others got there, they asked what I was doing.

"Ha, ha," I laughed. "I just got impaled by some thorns. Ha, ha." The Wilos thought it was pretty funny, too, and joined in the laughter.

But on the bright side, we were headed for home. I was alive. I had not been dismembered nor distressed beyond reason. I breathed a sigh of relief. Nothing else could possibly go wrong, so I was out of the woods, so to speak.

Which was when the outboard motor sputtered and died. The gas tank was empty. Oh yeah. How could I have forgotten about that possibility?

Floating slowly back home, I was left with the consolation of knowing that, if nothing else, I'd at least be able to eat of the fruit of my labor. I had speared a fish all by my little lonesome and, it being the first fish I had ever speared in this manner, it held some sentimental value. It wasn't just any old fish. It was a veritable trophy, a fine validation of my —

"Hey, Dah-wee," the Wilo in front of me turned and interrupted my musings, "I'm gonna take this little fish of yours and give you this big one of mine instead."

What! How could he make such a cruel and insensitive offer? Didn't he understand the sentimental significance of my little fish? I admit, I had worked up a substantial appetite during the course of the day's activities. Yes, that big juicy fish of his made mine look like something that had already been digested. But still, I could never...

Later that evening, frying up the nice big juicy fish in the frying pan, I reflected on how it is better to give than to receive. If I hadn't been willing to set aside sentimentality and part with my trophy fish, perhaps I would have offended that Wilo man. Perhaps it would have alienated him; made him think that I considered myself too good for his fish. Perhaps I would have gone to bed on an empty stomach.

Chapter 44

Diphthongs and Dieresis

Whoever says linguistical analysis can't be fun, has never spoken a more true word

I distinctly remember how happy I was to be done with school when after twelve long years, despite a resistant brain and a proclivity to daydream, I graduated top of my class. Home schooling is great that way. I didn't have long to catch my breath, however, as I promptly and unwittingly dove right back into a life that would be defined in large part by study. Why hadn't anybody warned me?

What I was learning a lot of now was vocabulary. I would have thought that after a lifetime of speaking English, I'd have most of the words down pat; but no. If someone had warned me that as a missionary I would be in danger of being exposed to words such as *archiphoneme* and *homorganic* and *vocoide* and *allophone* and *morphology* and *tagmeme*, well, I might have considered pursuing a line of work involving a little less technical jargon, like maybe rocket science.

Alas, once I entered missionary life, I was taken by surprise, ambushed by an implacable army of big words. In my leisure reading, I would occasionally stumble smack into a paragraph like:

Simply put, orthographical endeavor must be unambiguous, entailing both an etic and emic perspective of said language. The interpreting of suspicious and non-suspicious segments and sequences, separating CAE's from CIE's and segments from sequences, and determining which are MEE in their function, is essential. Note that diphthongs should be avoided and the need for dieresis will likely be limited. Of course, adjunct slots, referred to by ignorant laymen as clause root tagmemes, are inconsequential in this stage. Vocoides should pose little problem. Just remember that the IC of any given segment or sequence may influence blah blah blah...

What's up with that? Where do these words come from, and do they carry contagious diseases? Pressing on ahead with the naive assumption that such paragraphs were intended to be deciphered, I would read and reread them until eventually numbness would settle upon me and I would feel myself curling up into the protective fetal position.

One of the primary objectives of our missionary team was to develop an alphabet that would accurately represent the Wilo language. To arrive at that point, we had to focus a lot of our attention on completing the linguistical analysis of the Wilo language. This process entailed in-depth study of each distinct sound the language uses, determining which of those sounds would require their own letter in the alphabet, and what that letter should be.

No sweat. How hard could that be? Unfortunately, certain excessively intellectual individuals had taken it upon themselves to publish big, exhaustive (and exhausting, if you've ever tried to carry one) books explaining how one must go about doing this, confusing the issue with facts and rules and methods and stuff. Whatever happened to just going with your gut feeling? What's wrong with winging it?

Anyway, we brought out the books, followed all the rules, stuck with the methods, and waded through it all. We eventually finished the analysis and developed an alphabet for the Wilo language. We used symbols that most closely paralleled the Spanish alphabet, so that once a Wilo person learned to read and write in their own language, learning to do so in Spanish would not be such a huge jump, should they so desire.

Unfortunately, completing that task did not mean I had escaped all the big words. No, life being what it is, I still occasionally found myself involved in yet another jargon-filled technical powwow with my co-worker Phyllis, a certifiable linguistics junkie. It wouldn't take long for the numbness to set in, and I would drift off into a dream about being a rocket scientist. I would dream of packaging up all the big words, strapping them onto a rocket and sending it off in search of the *Mars Observer*.

Then Phyllis' voice would cut through my dream, bringing me back to reality, asking me if I'm OK, and why I'm beginning to curl up on the couch like that.

Chapter 45

Confessions of a Real Ladies' Man

The Fonz of Happy Days meets George of the Jungle

To tell you the truth, it's somewhat embarrassing. Normally I wouldn't even mention it because I'm uncomfortable bringing attention to my appealing qualities. Nevertheless, for posterity's sake I feel it best to shed momentarily my accustomed humility in favor of the more illuminating, unbiased facts as I perceive them.

You see, not long after arriving in Pakali it became apparent that – how can I put this humbly and delicately? – a number of young Wilo girls were quite obsessed with me. There, I said it.

It's true. Perhaps it could be attributed to my urbane, polished manner. Or maybe it was my shiny white skin and mysterious accent. I don't know. What I do know is that, whether walking down to the river, meandering throughout the village, or entering a house, I rarely failed to cause quite a stir among those of that particular demographic.

How was I so certain that these young ones were smitten with me? Well, it couldn't have been clearer had it been written in big blue block letters across a cloudless sky. Whenever I would stroll toward one of these girls, their eyes would be glued to my every move until I had made my way past them and well beyond. Some would stand frozen and stare up at me in a wide-eyed, disconcerted manner, while others would whisper things about me urgently to those around them. Indeed, the Fonz of *Happy Days* fame never elicited such enraptured reactions as I did in Pakali.

The youngest of my admirers would often coyly hide their true emotions behind a brilliant disguise of terror. Yeah, right. It might have been believable if they hadn't overdone it to such an extreme. I could see right through the façade. The older, more mature admirers, those who had already learned how to walk and talk a bit, were less dissimulating, at times being so forward as to tentatively delve into my personal life, asking questions like where I was going.

They were all taken with my sense of humor. My one-liners, even when I wasn't particularly trying to be funny, would often send them into gales of appreciative laughter. Such was their admiration that they would even call their friends over to hear me repeat what I had just said.

If you have ever seen the black-and-white footage of fans screaming and fainting at a single glimpse of the Beatles, then you can picture the kind of reception I often elicited from these girls.

I tried not to let it all go to my head, but it was hard being humble when virtual strangers would actually start shouting and practically swooning whenever I approached. Sometimes they would run home, impacted to the point of tears, no doubt to breathlessly tell of their close encounter with *moi*. At other times, with their large brown eyes they would simply cast me a "go thither" look, peeking out from behind their mother, overcome with shyness at my presence.

Someone with less insight might have assumed these children were reacting in fear. They certainly did put forth a convincing act. But I wasn't fooled. I may be many things, but delusional I am not. Just because someone runs off screaming, doesn't mean they are terrified, right? I mean, any number of emotions might produce that kind of behavior.

And just because all the parents of these young ones kept telling them that I was a cannibal and that I would take them away if they misbehaved, that doesn't mean that they actually believed it. Who would believe something like that about me? Not these adoring kids, that's for sure.

But familiarity does breed contempt, and I found that, as time passed, all my admirers began losing some of that enthusiasm. They stopped reacting to me and began treating me like I was just a normal person, sometimes even ignoring me completely.

I held up as best I could in the face of this demotion from superstardom to a has-been. But whenever visitors from other villages happened to pass through, I would approach them and the look of rapturous admiration in the eyes of the children would transport me back on the magic carpet of nostalgia to those early days when my many young admirers would scream and shout at the very sight of me. Ahh, for the good ol' days.

Chapter 46

Moving Up in the World

Home improvement comes to the jungle

In the late 1990s, much of the world's focus was on the upcoming new millennium. Out with the old, in with the new. In spite of living in a society that more closely resembled the thirteenth century, I found myself becoming somewhat caught up in this frenzy of updating and upgrading to receive the twenty-first century in style. I decided the time had come for me to get to work on a home-improvement project that had long been kept on hold. The time was ripe, I determined, to put up some real walls inside my house.

For the past seven years I had lived very simply, with few household conveniences. This was due in part to the fact that I resemble neither Tim the Toolman nor Bob the Builder. I can put up with a lot of inconvenience for a long time before I consider the situation untenable. It was also partly due to the fact that I had made a pact with myself that I would not put up interior walls in my house until I reached a reasonable degree of fluency in the Wilo language.

I should say that during those first seven years, I did have interior walls in my house, but they were an unsightly black color and were as thin as plastic. They were, in fact, unsightly black plastic walls.

These ascetic walls, while not esthetically pleasing, had served me well over the years, and they fit in fine with the decor of this little mud house that had no running water, no sinks and counters, no cupboards, no electrical outlets, no light switches, no interior doors. Bare bones.

But what better way to greet the new millennium than in a house with real cement-block walls! So I went to the corner building-supplies store and bought a bunch of cement blocks. Then I called up the local contractor and he took care of it from there. Oh... wait! Sorry. My dreams are intruding into this account.

There was no building-supplies store; no contractor. When I finally convinced myself that I should set aside a couple of weeks to do this home-improvement job, I wrote down a purchase list. I would need a few trowels, a couple of buckets, a level, bags of cement, a few bags of lime, and a big paintbrush.

But what good does a purchase list do in the jungle? Not much, unless you're needing to start a fire, or if you run out of toilet paper.

Fortunately, our missionary team extended well beyond the jungle. There was a support infrastructure in place that was set in action. Enter, stage left, the missionary pilot. When one of the airplanes landed in Pakali, I sent my purchase note out to town with him. Thanks, Pilot.

The pilot, though, had little time to be running around town buying the things on my list. That wasn't his contribution to the team. The pilots were generally up before the sun, preparing to spend the entire day either flying to the various mission stations, or doing the mechanical upkeep on the aircraft.

When the pilot landed the airplane in town, another missionary was there to meet him, a missionary whose responsibility was to organize and put together cargo for flights into the mission stations. He took the incoming cargo, passengers, and mail to the main office in town. My purchase note went with this missionary and was placed with other pieces of mail on a table. Thanks, Flight Cargo Administrator. Eventually the office secretary sorted the mail and put my note into the mailbox of the supply buyer. Thanks, Secretary.

At some point, the supply buyer checked his mailbox and found my note there. The job of the supply buyer was to attempt to decipher the purchase lists of missionaries living in isolated areas, go shopping, and then take the heat when the missionaries complained that he bought the wrong thing. He added my list to his list of lists, and prepared to go shopping. Thanks, Supply Buyer.

The supply buyer was a nice guy and all, but he wasn't about to buy the things I asked for out of his own wallet. He needed to get some money from me. And that's when the people in the finance office got involved. The finance people were tasked with the job of depositing and withdrawing money from each missionary's account whenever donations came in or expenses were incurred.

The finance people checked my financial account and then authorized the supply buyer to go out and spend a bunch of my money. Thanks, Finance People... I guess.

Once everything was purchased, it was loaded onto a commercial boat that passed by Pakali several times a year, and a couple of weeks later we were unloading the boat and hauling the hundred-pound bags of cement up to my house.

The next step in putting up walls in my house was to bring up mounds of sand from the river. We soon had a good supply of sand on hand, but before we could begin putting up the block walls, we had to have blocks. I had obtained a mold for making concrete blocks, so we set about mixing sand, cement and water into just the right consistency. We shoveled a little into the mold, tamped it down, flipped it upside down, carefully lifted the mold up and *voila*, our first concrete block was... a crumpled pile of cement and sand. Eventually we got the mixture right and our first block sat there majestically. Now all we had to do was repeat that routine a thousand more times.

A few of the tribal people wanted to learn how to make blocks, so they pitched in and helped. Once we had made a sufficient supply of blocks and they had cured and hardened in the sun, I was finally able to start putting up my walls. Who knew that home improvement in the jungle would be such an exercise in teamwork, tedium, and patience?

So it was that the new millennium found me comfortably

ensconced in my updated digs, enjoying the luxury of having rooms partitioned off with concrete block walls, and doors that opened and closed and swung on real hinges. Could the advent of kitchen cupboards be on the horizon? And how many people would be involved in *that* project?

Chapter 47

Eating Out

A tribal invitation to supper

Admittedly, I've taken no advanced courses in the sciences of hydrology, but in spite of my limited education in that field, I was fairly certain that the canoe coasting gently up to the riverbank was in open defiance of one of its foundational principles. It was so loaded down with passengers that it appeared to be locomoting below the water's surface.

The men in the canoe, understanding full well their precarious state, were sitting very still indeed as the river lapped hungrily at the top of the sideboards, impatient for the one false move that would allow it to pounce and swallow up the boat and its occupants.

It was the guys returning from fishing, so once I finished bathing I ambled over to peruse their take. By the time I got there they were lined up along an upside-down canoe, using it as a table to clean their catch. Lobeto looked up as I walked over, and asked, "Would you like me to bring you some fish later on? Or better yet, why don't you come by my house tonight and eat with us."

Sounded OK to me, so that night I headed to Lobeto's house. Along the way a girl spotted me and asked where I was going.

"I'm going to Lobeto's house to eat fish," I said.

"Oh." She did her best to sound uninterested but a couple of seconds later bolted down a narrow gap between two houses and disappeared around a third. It seemed she was to be the advance party that would announce my imminent arrival. Arriving at the door of Lobeto's house, I could hear her breathless announcement to the others congregated within. I hesitated briefly to allow her the opportunity to bask in the spotlight before its bright glare would be directed on me. I cleared my throat and in a loud voice said, "Should I come in?"

"Yes. Come in," a chorus of voices answered.

When I ducked through the door, I could see that a lot of people were seated around the fire. Most of them were sitting on pieces of wood on the ground; a few were sitting in hammocks.

One of the ladies immediately stood up and proffered me the rough-hewn pole she had been sitting on. "Here, sit down," she said.

Coming from a culture where the polite etiquette is for men to give up their chairs to women, this Wilo custom was a bit hard for me to adjust to. But she would have been offended had I gallantly refused, so I just took it and sat down, without saying thank-you, which is another Wilo custom that was hard to get used to. I hated not being able to say thank-you.

A sturdy stick had been pushed into the dirt floor in such a way that it was angled over the fire, and from it hung an aluminum pot with steam rising up into the thatched roof. From the moment I entered the house, a crowd of people had been forming around this pot and an enthusiastic discussion was now underway as they argued about which piece of fish would be best suited for me. When they had settled on just the right piece, it was scooped out of the pot along with some broth, and handed to me on a tin plate.

There weren't enough plates to go around, but that didn't stop everybody from eating. Those who didn't get a plate simply used a piece of cassava as their makeshift plate; a practical choice as the plate itself could then be eaten, thus reducing the amount of dishes to be washed. There were no spoons at all, so we ate the fish with our fingers and slurped up the broth.

The food was good, and the conversation would have been good too, except that everybody in the house was fascinated and preoccupied by the slowness with which I ate my piece of fish. They spent much of the mealtime commenting on it.

And indeed they had a point. I'm not a very skilled fish eater. I am reluctant to choke to death on a stray fishbone, so I carefully – the Wilos would say fastidiously – pick out the bones before inserting the fish into my mouth. The Wilos, on the other hand, have perfected the slurp method of eating fish. They can seemingly insert an entire fish into their mouth, make a couple of giant slurping sounds and pull out only the skeleton. It looked like a fun way of eating fish, but dangerous for a novice such as me.

Finishing up, I was shown where there was a small bowl with some soapy water in it for washing hands once the meal was done. A few people had already eaten and departed, but I stood there for a few moments, again feeling uncomfortable with a Wilo custom: that of eating and running. One of the ladies eventually took matters into her own hands. "Dah-wee, did you eat now?" she asked me pleasantly.

"Yes, it was good," I replied.

"Are you going home now?"

"Yeah, I'm going home now."

"OK, go home."

So I went home, without saying good-night, which is yet another of those Wilo customs that make me feel uncomfortable. But I repeat myself.

Chapter 48

Survival of the Fittest

Where are all the babies who are born with physical deformities?

If it is true that the measure of a hockey player is the number of teeth missing, then the Wilo tribe would have been able to field its very own professional league. It seemed almost everybody was missing a tooth or two, which wasn't surprising, considering that dental hygiene had only recently begun to be practiced in their villages, and that by only a few. Whether in their homes, at their gardens, or on the jungle trails, there always seemed to be much laughter and light-heartedness among the Wilos, so dental deficient smiles were a common sight.

Outside of this lack of pearly whites, however, there were very few physical deficiencies and deformities to be seen among the Wilos.

True, there was Nanisa, the elderly lady who couldn't stand upright. And there was the young lady who nimbly went about the village using a sturdy pole as a sort of crutch because she was missing a leg.

And there was the guy who had a scar on his leg where an irritable alligator had clamped onto him, and the boy who had a scar across his cheek where a fish-hook that was part of a fish-trap had raked across his face. There were myriad other scars and bumps to be seen on people young and old, male and female, the usual assortment of blemishes and trophies from life's unavoidable mishaps.

What we saw no sign of, though, were people living with birth defects. Where were the children suffering from a cleft palate, or a cleft lip, or a clubfoot, or a hand deformity? Surely in a setting so far from hospitals and medical treatment, these kinds of birth deformities would surface from time to time.

Judging by appearances, however, I would have assumed that every Wilo baby was born perfectly formed, every part of their tiny body intact and accounted for. Could that really be the case? The Wilos had many jungle remedies they used to treat everything from snake-bites to flu symptoms. Had they also stumbled across a natural pregnancy drug that caused all their babies to be born without defect?

Of course not. Truth be known, babies born with a visible birth defect, with something even as remediable as a cleft palate or a cleft lip, were allowed to live only long enough for someone to dig a shallow grave.

It wasn't that the Wilos thought physical deformities and irregularities in their society were unacceptable. Indeed, those who developed or acquired deformities after they were born were not ostracized in the least. But if a newborn baby was to survive its first few hours on earth, it had to be a normal-looking baby. This was not something that the Wilos required out of a sense of aesthetics. Rather, it was something that their spiritual beliefs required of them.

The Wilos believed that deformity in a newborn was the result of sinister spiritual activity. It was a spiritual taboo to allow such a child to live. They believed that if a pregnant woman were to look upon a baby born with a cleft lip, she in turn would give birth to a baby with the same deformity. In fact, even if she were to simply hear a description of the birth defect, the results would likely be the same. Their solution then, was to simply kill the baby before it was seen by another pregnant lady. For them, it was the responsible thing to do.

In this isolated tribal society, a society that many on the outside would naively consider to be idyllic and innocent, a scene practically right out of a horror movie was being replayed over and over again in real life each time a baby was born with a physical deformity. But the Wilos were not acting in malice when they killed their deformed babies. They were merely responding to culturally induced fears. Societal security required it. According to their perspective, the immorality would be to allow the baby to live and thus endanger the unborn babies of other pregnant women.

It shouldn't have surprised me, since fear is a common denominator of all human societies. Why would the Wilos be any different? And yet there was something of a difference. Whereas many societies are unaware of the fears that underlie their culture, the Wilos seemed to see it, and were holding out hope that the Bible would offer an alternative. I doubted they would be disappointed.

Chapter 49

Lamaze Class – Wilo Style

Wilo tips for pregnant ladies

Have you ever wondered why it is that some babies are born quickly, for all appearances desperate to escape the confines of the womb, while other babies dig in their heels and wear the mother out to the point of unconsciousness before grudgingly making their exit (or entrance, depending on your point of reference)?

Have you ever wondered what a rockhead fish, an armadillo, and a turtle have in common?

Have you ever wondered just what rockhead fish, armadillos, and turtles might have to do with child bearing?

If you answered yes to all those questions, you think altogether too much. Or you think like a Wilo.

Rockhead fish live – you guessed it – among rocks. They love to wedge themselves into tiny crevasses between rocks where predators are largely helpless to reach them. The Wilos, for their part, love eating these fish, and they spend entire days diving deep into the water to hook them out of their craggy sanctuaries. These fish are very difficult to dislodge from their hiding places.

The armadillo makes its home under the ground, burrowing fast and deep. Every now and then the Wilos would come across an armadillo in the jungle. A chase usually ensued, with the Wilos and their dogs attempting to grab the armadillo before it could find safety underground.

This was rarely a successful tactic, and the dogs, getting caught up in the euphoria of the pursuit, would sometimes follow the armadillo right into the hole in the ground. If the dogs were fortunate enough to return to the surface alive, they usually did so with their faces torn and bloodied. To extract an armadillo from the safety of its den the Wilos had to either dig fast, hard and deep, or flood the hole with water in order to force it out.

And then there's the turtle. They withdraw into their shell at the least sign of danger, and when they do come out, they show only their head, neck, and legs.

Turtle meat is a delicacy among the Wilos, and they would travel for days up tiny out-of-the-way tributaries and lagoons just to get a sackful of turtles. Getting the turtles into the boat wasn't too hard, but getting them out of the shell was another matter.

These three animals have a couple of things in common. They all show up on the menu of the Wilos, and they all put up quite a fight when being forcibly removed from the safety of their home. Once they're entrenched they're hard to evict.

Another thing they have in common is that, as food, they are all off limits to Wilo women who are pregnant. It is taboo for a pregnant woman to eat rockhead fish, armadillo, and turtle.

The Wilos believe that diet plays a substantial role in determining if childbirth will be quick and straightforward, or prolonged with many complications. There are some things a pregnant woman just shouldn't eat, because certain attributes of the animal she eats will then transfer over to the baby in her womb.

In the jungle, far from hospitals, the last thing a pregnant woman wants is for her baby to stubbornly refuse to exit at the appropriate moment. And the way to prevent this, they believe, is to simply avoid eating those animals that are known for their tendency to cling tightly to the safety of their home.

So the next time your unborn baby's lease is expired and yet he's refusing to be graciously evicted from the womb, think back to what you've eaten during the past nine months. That's what the Wilos would do.

Chapter 50

Two Babes in the Woods

A girl from Miami and a boy from Canada meet in the Amazon

I glanced at my watch and noted numbly that it had been five hours. I sat at the desk, my face creased in concentration. It was late afternoon, and a small twelve-volt fan was blowing hot air at me as I sat hunched over the two-way radio, my ear attuned to every nuance of the chirping sounds emanating from it. Hatred toward my fellow missionaries was brewing. Frustration had been mounting over the past several hours, but I was determined. Another opportunity would come soon – I just had to wait for it, be ready for it. Like a bird of prey suspended momentarily over a field-mouse before diving, my finger hovered purposefully over the "enter" key of a relic computer. With my free hand I wiped the perspiration from my brow and adjusted the fan which, ironically, seemed to provide relief from the heat only when I sweated.

There! A lesser person might have missed the miniscule change in the chirping that indicated the current transmission was ending. Without hesitation, my finger dived down and firmly struck the "enter" key. My eyes remained glued to the display panel of the radio tuner, silently imploring the needles to begin the rhythmic rise and fall that would signify success. Surely I had been quick enough this time. A brief silence ensued, a heavy, expectant silence similar to that which separates the bolt of lightning from the boom of thunder. When the chirping of the radio resumed, my shoulders sagged; I had been vanquished yet again. Apparently, lesser people were not at all common. Some other missionary at some other remote jungle location sitting at some other radio had inexplicably beaten me to the draw yet again. For the fifteenth time that afternoon I wondered, *How could this be?* Should I just give up?

I wasn't surprised that there was such stiff competition from the dozen or so other jungle-bound missionaries vying for this chance to communicate with the outside world, but still, did these people have nothing better to do than sit at their ham radios all afternoon? Obviously, everybody else who tuned into this frequency had me beat by a mile. I was little more than a babe in the woods by comparison, and I determined to develop a regimen of finger calisthenics to become more competitive in the future.

For now, though, keeping the white flag of surrender firmly tucked away, I reset the computer and again positioned my sissy finger over the "enter" key. I waited. Half an hour later the bird of prey again dived down, and this time I was rewarded with seeing the radio, the tuner, the modem, and the computer all spring to life as communication with the hub was mercifully established.

Finally. Take that, all you slow pokes out there! I should have collapsed in exhaustion, but instead I felt euphoric. Success! I had defeated the ene— Whoa. Deep breath. Count to ten – check. Think happy thoughts – check. Firmly secure Mr Hyde back inside the skin of Dr Jekyll – check.

This was PACKET. This was e-mail being sent and received via ham radio. This was our exit from the Jurassic age into the cyber. It was e-mail at a snail's pace of less than twenty bytes a second, but it sure beat the two-month cycle it generally took for traditional letters to leave the jungle and replies to arrive. Connection to the hub out in town was granted one at a time, and was on a first-come-first-served basis. The transmission was affected by inclement weather and the hub was susceptible to extended crashes, but even for a babe in the woods such as me, it was a wonderful technological advancement.

What made this primitive cyber communication all the more welcome to me in particular was the fact that I had recently come across a babe in the woods of a different sort. The Bible says that every good gift, and every perfect gift is from above, so I suppose it shouldn't have surprised me that she came down from the sky and landed within a stone's throw of my mud house, not that I was inclined to throw any when I saw her.

The airplane had just landed on our jungle airstrip, and as I exited my house and made my way to meet the visitors who were disgorging from the small aircraft, there she was. In spite of the fact that Marie hailed from the concrete jungle of Miami, she didn't look out of place at all in my neck of the woods. She was swatting nonchalantly at the gnats that clouded around her, and her golden-brown eyes returned the curious gazes of the Wilos who had come out to meet the plane.

She and the others traveling with her stayed in Pakali only for a few days. She and I didn't interact much at all, but unbeknownst to me, a time-delayed spark had been planted. A few months later Marie accepted an invitation to come teach Spanish to a group of newly arrived missionaries. She was still several hundred miles away from Pakali village, but at least we were now in the same country.

An immense jungle, inhospitable mountain ranges, and mile after mile of rugged terrain lay between us, but my thoughts, impervious to such barriers, often visited her. It wasn't long after her return that I began feeling the effects of distraction. The profitable study of verbs and adjectives and discourse-level grammar that had been my focus over the past few years began to be usurped by an inclination to stare vacantly at the wall and a proclivity for leafing randomly and blindly through pages of vocabulary and grammatical charts. I wasn't getting much work done.

I seemed to have little trouble finding the time and motivation to write volumes of letters, though. Some were written on paper and sent out with an airplane whenever one happened to pass through, while others were composed on the old computer and sent via PACKET. Both systems could accurately be described as snail mail.

Distraction grew into obsession, and over time I had to confront the realization that my mind had been completely and irretrievably derailed. Try as I might, I just couldn't seem to get back on track.

Over the course of the next three years, that spark that had so surreptitiously been planted would burst into flame, then would be doused, only to once again be rekindled. Eventually, the time came to let our missionary community in on what I assumed to be a little secret, although I was to find that no one was at all surprised. The beat-up computer, the modem, the radio tuner and the chirping radio sprang to life, transmitting the following press release:

In this day and age of failed corporate mergers, hostile takeover bids, volatile markets, and unpredictable investment returns, there is not a whole lot of great news being broadcast.

However, Federal Reserve Chairman Alan Greenspan's warnings against it notwithstanding, I'd like to indulge in a bit of irrational exuberance in announcing an upcoming merger that appears quite promising. In a non-hostile takeover bid, the Davey Jank Company recently proposed to the Marie Correa Corporation that they combine their assets, such as they are, and launch a new company under a single banner that would be better suited to meet the needs of the twenty-first century.

According to statements made during a recent interview, Mr Davey Jank believes that the proposed merger would greatly enhance the effectiveness of these two companies and improve both the workplace and employee morale on the job because of the qualities the Correa Corporation brings to the negotiating table. When asked what positive qualities the Jank Company would contribute to the mix, Mr Jank appeared momentarily confused and at a loss for a reply. He eventually managed to mumble that he had no comment on that.

"I have no comment on that," he mumbled.

The proffered proposal by the Davey Jank Company was taken into consideration by the single member of the Marie Correa board of directors and was passed unanimously. Pending a certain amount of time to put the wheels in motion, the combined companies hope to launch their new endeavor sometime in the month of July, although as yet no exact date has been set.

A top executive at the Davey Jank headquarters, who wishes to remain anonymous, stated that presently his company is doing little more than basking in the approval of the proposal. He hastened to add however, that he expected there to be on-going negotiations in the future to determine just what the power sharing structure of the new company will be. Nevertheless, it is anticipated that the Jank/Correa Company will be able to generate good revenue and show a long-term profit in spite of the forecasted adjustments that are common during such transition periods.

Chapter 51

So Davey Married an Axe Murderer

Why would such a thing be said about the new missionary?

At least, that's the general gist of what some of the more irascible toddlers of the village were being told by their parents.

An axe murderer? That sounded pretty scary, and that was precisely its purpose. Not that the Wilo children were afraid of sharp instruments, mind you. At a very early age all of them were educated on the practical uses of knives, machetes, and axes, and on their inherent dangers as well. Their teacher was most often the blade itself, a very effective, if at times unforgiving, educator.

But as a result, these Wilo children quickly grew to be adept in the art of cutting and chopping, which is a good thing, since knives, machetes, and axes are central to the Wilo lifestyle. Machetes in particular are a common accessory of the Wilo wardrobe. Machetes are to the Wilos what kilts are to Highland Scots: they'd feel naked without one.

Murder, on the other hand, was a very scary thing for the Wilos to contemplate. Theirs was a society where murder was practically unheard of. In fact, it was far more likely that an angry person would commit suicide than that they would commit murder.

So what was going on? Why was it not uncommon for me to hear a mother tell her child, "See Marie? Look at her! She's going to cut you up into little bits and throw the pieces into the jungle!" Why would they even think to say that? Did they actually believe that it might be true?

As with many other puzzling things about the Wilos, the

answer was to be found in their culture. Wilo parents wouldn't discipline their children by grounding them for the weekend, or by making them sit in the corner, or by giving them a timeout. They wouldn't spank their children, although if sufficiently provoked they might pick up a flexible twig and attempt to strike them with it.

No, instead of inflicting pain or inconvenience upon their children, they much preferred to instill fear in them. And what could be more scary to a child than to hear that the new lady in the village standing quietly nearby is a mutilation just waiting to be perpetrated!

So with the arrival of Marie, some enterprising Wilo parents saw an opportunity to exploit the fact that she was an unknown quantity, particularly in the eyes of the children. Whenever a child was misbehaving and Marie happened to be nearby, they would urgently point at her and tell the child to stop it, or else that white woman would come for them.

They scared their children as a way of keeping them in line. And besides, they all seemed to enjoy the spectacle of the child breaking into terrified wailing upon hearing of the impending doom.

Come to think of it, I vaguely remember parents often pointing me out to their children when I first arrived at the village. I had thought they were just saying to them, "Hey, look! Here comes that nice missionary. Don't cry, child. He won't hurt you."

Unfortunately for the parents in the village, this disciplinary strategy ultimately proved ineffective, or at the best temporary, as most children quickly caught on to this particular ploy. The more the children got to know us and interact with us, the less gullible they became to suggestions that we and the Grim Reaper were one. Eventually it got to the point that, when breathlessly told of our supposed evil intentions toward them, the children would merely smile the smile of someone who has finally come to know better and is no longer afraid.

Sadly, Wilo children were inculcated with many other fears as well, fears that didn't subside over time, but rather intensified as they grew into adulthood. Their spiritual beliefs revolved around the concept of fear: fear of the evil spirits, fear of the witchcraft of others, fear of the dead, fear of being helpless in the face of spiritual attack.

Many of them were holding out hope that the Bible would provide an element of freedom from this constant oppression of fear. They wouldn't be disappointed. We looked forward to the day when both child and adult alike could smile the smile of someone who has finally come to know better and is no longer afraid.

Chapter 52

Me and My Shadow

Allow me to introduce you to the deviant cousin of Murphy's Law

Soccer (or *futbol*, as it is referred to in the Spanish-speaking world) is a staple entertainment among many of the tribal groups in the Amazon, including the Wilos. Long before we ever came on the scene, they had begun incorporating *futbol* into the fabric of their society. For us missionaries it was an activity that provided a great avenue for informal interaction with them, whether as players or as spectators. For the Wilo players it provided an opportunity to run circles around the panting missionaries.

Futbol is not only a village activity; it is also an inter-village, and sometimes even an inter-tribal activity. Teams and spectators from one village often travel to other villages to compete in *futbol* and *futbolito*, a more intense kind of soccer played with a team of five on a miniature pitch.

So we weren't surprised when the Wilos mentioned their plans to visit a village upriver for an afternoon of games. We decided to go along with them, and in festive spirit we all piled into the boat. With the sputtering outboard motor pushing the overloaded dugout canoe, it would take us two hours to get there.

Navigating the treacherous waters of the Balawa River at night during dry season was something to be avoided at all costs, so the plan was to arrive at the upriver village, play a couple of *futbol* matches, then leave at roughly 4:00 p.m. in order to arrive safely home before dark.

Amazingly, the person who had come up with this optimistic itinerary had inexplicably failed to take into account the fact that I was going along. Had he never been on a river trip with me before? Indeed he had. He should have realized that with his optimistic assumptions that all would go as planned, he was virtually laughing in the face of a phenomenon that often shadows me on river trips. This phenomenon, which I shall refer to as My Shadow, is a withering force for evil that at times makes even Murphy's Law seem accommodating and ingratiating by comparison.

Not surprisingly, My Shadow lost little time in making its presence felt. We had barely pulled away from the shore when the previously mentioned beat-up old outboard motor shut off. Someone said it was sitting up so high on the backboard that the propeller was partially out of the water. We paddled the boat to the riverbank and one of the guys grabbed a machete and chopped a deep notch into the backboard so the motor would rest lower. I wasn't too sure what the boat owner was going to think about that one.

While this adjustment to the backboard was being made, I noticed a long, rather large crack in the boat through which water was flowing in quite freely. I pointed this out to some of the passengers but nobody seemed too concerned. One of them threw a small plastic container my way and I began the tedious but comforting task of keeping the river out of the boat.

We eventually got underway again. Two hours later we still had not arrived at our destination. But rounding a bend in the river, we saw a solitary man standing on the shore watching us curiously. We pulled up to the riverbank to visit for a bit. The piece of wood that was my chair had by this time made an indelible and somewhat painful impression upon me and I was more than happy to take advantage of this opportunity to get up and stretch.

Everybody disembarked and a few of the guys asked the man if he had anything to eat. He seemed delighted to have been asked, and off we went, an entire soccer team, to eat this poor man's food.

He took us to his house. On a rack above his cooking fire were about twenty smoked fish. He generously handed each of us one, thus depleting his stash considerably. I felt conflicted about being complicit in this grand larceny and gluttony, but I had learned by this time that when I insisted on adhering to my own sense of decorum, I often wound up offending someone. I took the fish I was proffered.

As I followed the rest of the team back to the boat I gnawed on the tough fish and hoped the man wouldn't forever hate us for having raided his kitchen with such enthusiasm. Then I heard him come busting out of his house yelling something. His tone instilled in me a sense that I should sprint back to the boat as expeditiously as possible, but I resisted. Instead I turned around.

He was waving something at us, and I was relieved to see it wasn't a shotgun. In his hand was a big pot of piping-hot banana soup. Apparently he didn't want us to leave without dessert.

We finally arrived at our destination only to find that many of the players from there had gone fishing. We sat around for a while watching the precious minutes tick by. When the fishermen returned, we wasted little time in playing our matches.

We were well behind schedule, and the sound of the final whistle had barely reached our ears before we were saying our quick goodbyes. We rushed down to the boat, throwing furtive glances over our shoulders at the sinking sun and advancing storm-clouds.

About an hour into our return trip it got dark, and navigation through the treacherous sandbars and boulders was left to memory alone. At least the riverbanks were still distinguishable in the starlit night. We clipped along at an exuberant pace for a while, with a reckless abandon that left my nerves a trembling mass quivering in the pit of my stomach. Boulders would loom up in front of us out of the darkness and the driver would swerve madly to avoid the unpleasantness of a head-on collision.

Then it began to rain, further limiting visibility while at the same time increasing the level of overall discomfort. I glanced back to check on the driver. Through the darkness I could see that he was doing fine, squinting against the rain and chatting with the person seated beside him.

I saw a brief glow, and realized he was drawing deeply on a cigarette he had purchased at the other village. I was dismayed – indeed, alarmed – at his total disregard for healthy living, his disdain for his well-being and that of the rest of us as well. The glowing cigarette butt was dangling precariously above the gas tank and oily water in the bottom of the boat. This was not a happy sight. My quivering nerves gave one last spasm and passed out.

Meanwhile, in the front of the boat the navigator was sitting in the prow, indicating to the driver which way to go by waving a dim flashlight into the night sky. It wasn't long before the inevitable happened as the navigator wasted little time indicating the boat right over a shallow rock. The subsequent *crunch* and high-pitched whine of the motor, followed by dead silence, was not a pleasant sequence of sounds. Our momentum carried us over the rock and we floated down the river for a while. The man formerly known as the navigator wisely kept silent as everybody enthusiastically pelted him with insults. We floated until we pushed up against a few boulders.

With about ten minutes of tinkering, the motor was back up and running, and we were good to go. As the lights of home came into view My Shadow wearily wiped its brow and began preparing for the next river trip.

Chapter 53

Flying Popcorn

When Wubadus come popping out of the ground like popcorn

If you're like me, then you are of the opinion that the study of fine cuisine and the study of ants should be always and forever mutually exclusive. It only makes sense. I found, however, that the Wilos harbored no such opinion, and this prompts me to share with you the sad plight of the Wubadu.

For much of the year the Wubadu maintain a discreet, rather low profile. They spend most of their time industriously pursuing their favorite pastime: that of digging winding tunnels and large holes underground. They do this with such enthusiasm and singleness of purpose that one is left to conclude they are preparing for a major jail break, which actually isn't too far from the truth.

In the dark reaches of the underground, the Wubadu are allowed to go about their preparations unobserved and ignored by the rest of the world. The light of day is shed briefly on their surreptitious activities only at such times as an errant foot or a wayward wheel breaks through the surface above them and disrupts their activity, much to their consternation and surprise.

Such unexpected and unintended insertions into Wubadu territory tend to elicit a good many startled expletives and frantic damage control, but the Wubadu, imperturbable and focused as always, ignore all the hubbub and simply dig down deeper, patiently biding their time.

Their time, such as it is, is heralded by nothing less than what appears to be the sprouting of wings! Thus endowed, and determined to make the most of it, their little underground world of tunnels and caverns understandably becomes quite constricting. Really, who would want to share tunnel space with other novice fliers intent on showing off their new wings? It's time, they decide, to take their show on the road, to the great upstairs, where they can really cut loose and stretch their wings.

Many of the Wubadu are familiar with the great upstairs. They've gone on forays, usually under cover of darkness, to forage for food up there.

Unfortunately for the Wubadu, they are not the only ones who forage in the great upstairs. This desire to fly free under the bright blue sky spells impending disaster for them; destruction and havoc. Horrible things await them upstairs. They do not realize it, but the foragers are about to become the foraged.

Upon exiting the dark confines of their tunnels, those fortunate ones who have sprouted wings take to the skies while the remainder content themselves with scurrying about on the ground for no apparent reason, although a casual observer might assume they are attempting to achieve lift-off through sheer speed alone.

Truth be told, even those Wubadu with wings don't do too well at flying. They spend most of their time and expend much of their energy careering laboriously from one bush to another, to all appearances panting profusely but undeterred.

It doesn't take long for them to draw an appreciative crowd. Wilo children and adults alike come hurrying over excitedly, each with a container of some sort, as the foraging begins. The Wubadu, understandably irate, object to being foraged and display their sharp displeasure by inserting their formidable pinchers into any and all foreign flesh.

An interesting battle ensues, during which the predominant sound is the delighted laughter of children, occasionally interrupted by their not-so-suppressed gasps of pain. The Wubadu, it should be noted, have an oversized head the size of a pencil eraser, and are quick to employ corresponding pinchers. To further complicate the plight of the human foragers, the Wubadu are not possessed of the let-go gene. Thus, to extricate oneself from their painful embrace is to effect the removal also of one's own cherished flesh.

When darkness falls, the Wubadu retreat back to their subterranean refuge. The next day, ever the optimists, their desire to fly once again overcomes common sense, and so the previous day's scenario replays itself. And the next day, again. And the day after that.

Finally, having suffered heavy casualties, and disillusioned with the great upstairs, the Wubadu are saved from extinction only when they grudgingly give up flying and return to digging their tunnels underground. Preparations are immediately put in motion for their next hurrah.

Meanwhile in the great upstairs, the Wilos content themselves with licking their wounds and tasting of the spoils of victory. For several days after, they continue to frequent the battle zone, much like the hungry hand frequenting the empty popcorn bowl, but eventually they too return to their normal life and await the next great escapade of the Wubadu.

Chapter 54

I'd Like to Buy an "S"

Freedom of speech means being able to tack an "s" onto the end of a word

No matter what those in authority might say about me, I'm not anti-authoritarian. I'm not opposed to structure and rules. But really, some rules are just plain bad. Some rules are so burdensome that no one, particularly innocent outsiders, should be held accountable to meet their stringent requirements. These are rules that cry out to be trodden underfoot; evil taskmasters who maliciously impose impossible standards in order to mock us and gloat at our futile attempts to conform.

Of course, rebellion is always an option when confronted with such tyrannical rules, and I was quite surprised and somewhat disappointed by the fact that the entire Wilo tribe had not yet risen up in protest, with one voice demanding fair and equitable treatment in regard to one particular rule that greatly troubled me as I went about learning the Wilo language.

This rule of which I speak was of such pervasive and perverse character that indeed I was often rendered speechless. Surely the Wilos themselves felt the same oppression and heavy burden placed upon them by this merciless rule.

But no, as I looked around me, it became evident the Wilos were, by some miracle, oblivious to the absurdity of the demands of this rule. They seemed perfectly content to allow this draconian structure to hold sway over something extremely vital to their culture: namely their speech.

The rule to which I refer is the one that dictates how to go about pluralizing nouns. Freedom of speech, in my mind, is the freedom to simply tack the letter "s" onto the end of a noun to pluralize it. I'm even willing to live with a few exceptions to the rule.

The Wilos enjoyed no such freedom. When it came to pluralizing nouns, they were all held under the bondage of a grammatical rule so fiendish and terrible that, given the chance, even the United Nations might unanimously vote to sanction it.

"So, what's the big deal? How hard can the silly rule be?" you might mock.

Allow me to explain. First, let us consider how the Wilo language goes about pluralizing animate objects (things that are living). The key to knowing how to pluralize animate nouns is to focus on the length of the word and the letter it ends with in its singular form.

For instance, if you wish to pluralize a word that is only one syllable long and ends with the letter *a* (with the exception of words ending with *iya*, *uwa*, or *uya*), or if it is a two-syllable word that ends in *e*, the entire word must take on a nasal quality and the final letter must be changed to the letter *o*. But if the word is one or two syllables long and ends in *o* or *u* or *i* (with the exception of words ending with *lo*, *wo*, and *yu*), or, if it is a three-syllable word ending in *e*, the entire word must take on a nasal quality and the final letter must be changed to the letters *do*.

On the other hand, if the word happens to end with the vowel combination *iya*, the only change that has to be made to pluralize the word is to replace the final two letters with the single letter *o*.

When the word ends with *uwa* or *uya*, the final syllable is deleted and a nasal quality is added to the remainder of the word. When the word ends with *lo* or *wo* or *yu*, pluralization is achieved by adding a nasal quality to the whole word.

When the word ends with *bo* and is pronounced with a nasal quality, and isn't a two-syllable word, the final syllable is replaced with *edo*.

When the word ends in *so* and is pronounced with a nasal quality, the final syllable is deleted.

By now most of the ambassadors at the United Nations would

be asking for a recess and a strong drink. But you and I know that we've only mentioned those rules that apply to animate objects. Let's move on to another category, shall we? Let's look at how to pluralize inanimate objects, things such as trees, rocks, and houses. It's much more straightforward.

For inanimate objects, if you wish to pluralize a word that ends with the letter *a*, you replace that letter a with the letters *iya*.

If, on the other hand you want to pluralize a word that ends with the letter *o*, you must replace that letter *o* with the letters *ihu*.

To pluralize any other inanimate nouns, you simply add the letters *biya* to the end of the word.

And that pretty much sums it up, except to say that, similar to English, there will be a few exceptions to the rules.

I hope you agree that a rule such as this should be universally condemned. The Wilos, sadly, seemed perfectly content to live with the brutal demands this rule placed upon them. Everybody from children playing at the river to gray-haired senior citizens socializing under the shade of a tree, seemed to have no problem adhering to it.

If Pat Sajak and Vanna White ever take their game show *Wheel of Fortune* to the jungle village of Pakali, I know what letter I'll ask for. "Yes, Pat, you heard right," I will say. "I don't care what it costs. I'd like to buy an 's'."

Chapter 55

Green Parrot Versus White Man

Who knew that outsmarting a bird could be so satisfying?

With a gentle bump, the prow of the boat rode up onto the muddy riverbank and we all sat still for a moment before disembarking. It was eerily quiet. None of the villagers were at the river, which seemed unusual. Normally someone would be washing their clothes, or children would be frolicking like otters in the water. This just didn't feel right.

I gingerly stood and stepped onto the clay of the riverbank. The three Wilos I was traveling with followed suit and together we made our way down a vague trail that led toward the houses. From all appearances the village was deserted. No dogs barked, no murmur of voices came from the dilapidated houses. Visitors to these areas usually were big news, attracting people from every corner of the village, but we walked alone from one vacant house to another.

At the time, I wasn't overly concerned. I was actually relieved that we did not have to fend off a pack of protective, toothy village dogs. It was not until later, when I had the opportunity to interpret this strange and unusual silence through the corrective lens of hindsight, that I realized the silence that met us at this remote village was of the sinister sort.

We made our way through the village until we came to a circular house with a cone-shaped thatched roof. A bleary-eyed dog lying near the entrance watched us warily, perhaps trying to determine if we posed a danger to his master, but more likely making sure we didn't step on him as we ducked through the doorway and into the darkness of the house.

I should have realized the dog's passive behavior was simply a ploy to lure me inside, but I was oblivious to the warning signs. Like a lamb led to the slaughter, I stepped past the dog and into the house, where a character practically taken right from the pages of an Alfred Hitchcock novel awaited this unsuspecting visitor.

It took a few seconds for my eyes to adjust to the darkness of the house. A small window provided sadly inadequate light and practically no ventilation. Near the center of the room a small fire was crackling, causing the shadows in the house to dance eerily about.

I eventually saw that several ragged hammocks with corresponding mosquito nets were hanging in one corner (assuming a round house is allowed corners), and a middle-aged man sat in one of them, repairing a fish spear.

He greeted us without much enthusiasm, but eventually stood up and cleared some clutter off a pole on the ground and suggested we sit down. I was proffered a small wooden bench; nothing seemed out of the ordinary. I sat down, and in doing so unwittingly took yet another step into the trap being set for me.

The man pushed some firewood further into the fire and it flared up, momentarily illuminating what seemed to be a crude storage platform hanging from the roof above me. The room in general was nondescript, which prevents me from describing it in any detail.

The lady of the house appeared out of the smoke and darkness, dipped some water from a container into an aluminum pot, and nestled the pot on the fire. She was going to make a hot palm-fruit drink for us. We sat and didn't say much.

Suddenly, a spool of fishing line thudded to the floor at my feet, narrowly missing my head. The Wilo people in the house found this very amusing, and initially so did I, until I heard the sinister laugh of the culprit himself. He was hiding on top of the storage platform above me. With a humorless chuckle he joined in the laughter and then began muttering unintelligibly.

It wasn't long before he extended his head over the platform and peered down at me from above, perhaps to see what damage he had caused, more likely to get a better fix on his target.

He was a big parrot with, as best I could see, a gimpy leg. Not very bright, as far as parrots go – just a uniform dark military green.

Our host, a man named Mosquito, put down the spear he was working on and shooed the bird away to another part of the house, perhaps fearing for my safety. The parrot squawked with indignation and I instinctively knew I would have to keep my eye on him. Some sixth sense was telling me that I would do well to monitor his every move.

Conversation continued amongst us humans. As we talked, Mosquito's wife busied herself with the process of preparing our palm-fruit drink. She had both hands up to her elbows in the pot of hot water and was pressing the meat off the palm fruits and then scooping the marble-sized seeds out. What remained in the pot was what we would drink. I wondered briefly where her hands had been recently, but then wrestled my thoughts into a happier corner.

Everything was so comfortingly normal that I allowed myself to drop my guard and almost missed seeing the big green parrot limp furtively to the wall and climb up the bamboo slats until he reached a pole that crossed over to the platform above me. I followed his progress out of the corner of my eye while attempting to appear as though I were giving full attention to the conversation. I must have been successful in this, because no one else seemed to notice the parrot.

He quietly made his way back onto the platform, and I was dismayed to see him immediately set about worrying the rope knot upon which the entire platform hung suspended high in the air. Was no one else cluing in to this? Were the evil machinations of this steely-eyed bird not obvious to all? Beads of sweat broke out on my brow. It was getting rather hot inside the house.

I couldn't take it anymore. When I saw that he was actually succeeding in loosening the knot, I stood up quickly and everybody in the house looked at me, startled. I made a show of stretching my legs, and meandered over toward a tiny window as though interested in something outside. Call me paranoid, but I needed to get out from under that storage platform. The gimpy bright-eyed parrot was making me nervous.

I looked out the window, following through with my little charade. A couple of seconds later a horrible crashing sound reverberated throughout the hut, accompanied by a cloud of dust and punctuated by the startled squawk of the parrot. I turned around and saw that the entire platform and all its contents had come crashing down on top of the wooden bench where I had sat only moments before.

Once again laughter filled the room. Through the dust and feathers I caught a glimpse of a dark green figure limping quickly behind some firewood stacked against the wall. He swiveled his head and looked in my direction one last time. I thought I saw a look of deep disappointment and defeat in his beady little eye. That's right, parrot. You lose. White man: one. Green parrot: zero. Who knew outsmarting a bird could be so satisfying?

Chapter 56

Don't Dis the Article

A key to effective storytelling in the Wilo language

If you're reading this, you probably are a fluent English speaker. At some point you've likely told a story or two in English. That being the case, here's a question for you: How does the English language mark the introduction of a new person or participant into a story in such a way that it is clear you're not referring to someone you've already made mention of? What is the grammatical rule that dictates this small but indispensable aspect of storytelling?

Most native English speakers would have difficulty even just understanding the question, much less coming up with a quick answer. But that is not to say that you don't instinctively follow the rule.

It's actually quite simple. It's all about the article of speech. Primarily, we use the article "a" when referring to a new character, and we use the article "the" when referring to a previously mentioned character. We do this naturally, unaware that we're following an important rule of deeper discourse for the English language.

For instance, assume I'm in the middle of recounting one of those on-the-edge-of-your-seat stories and I say, "So then the bear lunged out of the woods, lumbered over to me, and shook my hand."

Now, if I haven't previously introduced any bear into my story, there will be a lot of puzzled looks. People will say, "Huh? What bear? You never mentioned no bear!" The story will have lost its momentum and I'll be forever branded a poor storyteller.

If, on the other hand, I change the article and say, "So then *a* bear lunged out of the woods, lumbered over to me, and shook my hand", then everybody will simply accept the bear as a new – if strangely friendly – participant in the story and everything will make sense and flow right along, even though I don't come right out and say that the bear is one that is just now coming onto the scene. The listener understands that the phrase "a bear" implies that it is a character I am only now introducing into the story.

It's a little disconcerting to think that these two rather puny, under-appreciated articles of speech pack such a wallop in our language. They're low profile but high impact. These little words play an important role in communicating those unspoken yet crucial tidbits of information found throughout stories told in English. They also provide for us an example of the many subtle underpinnings that support effective communication in any language.

But why should we as missionaries even care about how to tell stories effectively? What's the point? It's not as through telling stories is a big part of missionary work. Or is it?

There is, for instance, the story of creation. There is also the story of the flood, the account of the life of Abraham, and of Joseph, and of Moses. There is the story of the birth, life, death, and resurrection of Jesus. There is the story of the early church, of the apostle Paul. Much of the Bible is presented in story form. In translating the Bible, we are in reality often translating stories; true stories of how God has interacted with man throughout the ages.

As we prepared to begin translating the Bible into the Wilo language, it was necessary that we uncover and then emulate the storytelling patterns the Wilo language employed.

How do the Wilos introduce a new character into a story? Not in the same way English does, that's for sure. The Wilo language doesn't even have articles of speech like "a" and "the".

Part of our focus in learning the Wilo language was to investigate these deeper areas of communicating large pieces of information. How does a Wilo formulate and present a convincing argument? How does he weave a primary thought throughout a paragraph? How does he add background information into his story without having it be confused with the principal story-line? Does the good guy always get introduced before the bad guy? Is the direct object handled differently when it has previously been the subject? The list goes on and on.

These are things that go beyond your typical grammar and vocabulary. Rather, they are the grease that allows many sentences to fit together friction-free when a speaker wishes to communicate on a deeper discourse level, interrelating many phrases. Communicating the gospel to the Wilos was going to require a large degree of fluency in their language. The ability to tell stories would indeed be vital.

Chapter 57

Off with Their Heads!

A rash, a magic marker, and some bumbling witchcraft

"Dah-wee, are you sitting there?" Bakala asked, as he and Labeto approached the door. They knew I was sitting there, because they were looking through the window at me. Though this was a common way for the Wilos to say "Knock, knock," I was often tempted to respond with, "No, I'm getting a bath down at the river," or some other sarcastic statement, but such a reply would have been more perplexing than funny to them.

"Yes, I'm sitting here. Come in," I said.

They came in and sat at the table and we talked about the weather and the village. These two young men didn't normally come just to visit, and I knew that eventually they would get around to the reason they were there.

"Do you have a magic marker?" Bakala asked. "If you do, we'd like to borrow it."

I went to my desk to see if I had one. "What do you want to use it for?" I asked curiously as I returned with the marker. No one had ever asked to borrow one before.

"Kwado is sick. We want to use the magic marker to heal her," he said.

Kwado is the Wilo word for "Grandma", and that is what all the elderly ladies of the village were often called. In this case I could guess which Kwado they were referring to. In one of the houses on the other side of the airstrip, an elderly lady had been sick for quite some time. An angry rash had broken out and covered her head, neck, and shoulders. It was very painful, and she was suffering quite a bit.

She had no intention of getting on that noisy flying contraption and being taken to a hospital in town. Medicines hadn't done much against the rash, and all the jungle remedies the Wilos tried on her hadn't had the desired effect either. So now these two young men were going to try to heal her. That was nice of them. But with a magic marker?

I gave them the marker and asked if I could come along. Their faces brightened. "Yes. Let's go," Bakala said with a smile.

I followed them down the trail to Kwado's house. Ducking through the low doorway, we stepped inside, and through the darkness and smoke we could see Kwado lying in her hammock in the far corner. She painfully sat up when she realized she was to be the object of our visit.

The two young men were chomping at the bit to get the healing process underway, but they soon realized they were still lacking a vital piece of equipment. They began searching desperately throughout the dark confines of the house. They unearthed a few loose sheets of paper, but after some discussion discarded them as useless. They looked inside baskets and behind stacks of firewood. After several frantic minutes of rooting about – *eureka!* – they found just what they were looking for: a ragged cardboard box.

They ripped the box into two pieces. Setting aside the longer piece, they approached Kwado with the marker and the smaller piece of cardboard clutched in their hands.

I still had no idea what they were about to do, but judging from the expression of equanimity on Kwado's emaciated face, she wasn't overly concerned. Perhaps she had been briefed on the proposed procedure.

They wrapped the cardboard gently around Kwado's head. Labeto held it in place, bringing to mind the image of a poor man's crown being placed on the head of an elderly queen. Meanwhile, Bakala took the marker and proceeded to draw something on the cardboard crown. He was quite meticulous, deliberately drawing a long squiggly oval. He filled the oval with dots and – just like that! – he had drawn a snake. His fellow healer murmured approval of the drawing, so he drew another snake, and then another, until a line of snakes was drawn around the entire circumference of the crown.

Bakala then produced a pair of scissors, and while the cardboard was still held in place against Kwado's head, he carefully cut through the cardboard until the head of one of the snakes was severed. He looked over at me and explained that this was a very dangerous procedure. If he were to accidentally cut through the entire width of cardboard, or if he were to mistakenly cut through the tail of one of the snakes, the procedure would not meet with success; Kwado would not get better. In fact, any such careless deviation from the proper procedure would likely result in her untimely death. It had to be done just right.

He proceeded to sever the head of each of the other snakes he had drawn as well. With the last snip, the cardboard was removed from Kwado's head and tossed aside. But that was not the end of this healing ritual. The second piece of cardboard was immediately wrapped around Kwado's emaciated shoulders, and once again the marker was brought out. But Bakala wasn't going to draw snakes on this piece of cardboard. Instead he would attempt to draw a sequence of frogs.

I soon sensed that something wasn't going right for the healers. After making several aborted attempts at drawing a frog, Bakala gave up and passed the marker to his cohort. Unfortunately, Labeto's attempts ended in failure as well.

They removed the cardboard from Kwado's shoulders and found a piece of scrap paper on which to practice. Labeto drew something and Bakala laughed and said, "No, that looks like a turtle." After a second attempt, he said, "That one looks like a rat." By now even Kwado was chuckling at their desperate predicament. Try as they might, they just couldn't draw anything resembling a frog.

Labeto looked up at me, hope dawning in his eyes. "Dah-wee, can you draw a frog?"

I had never expected my complete lack of artistic ability to come in so handy. I was already feeling somewhat conflicted about – if not exactly complicit in – this little healing ritual that smacked of novice witchcraft.

"No, I don't know how to draw a frog," I said honestly, although my tone of regret was a little less than honest.

For several more minutes the two healers continued experimenting with the marker until finally they were satisfied with their ability to draw an image that sufficiently resembled a frog. Once again Labeto held the cardboard against Kwado's shoulders, and Bakala drew frogs on it from one end to the other, just as he had done with the snakes. Out came the scissors and in no time at all the frogs were also decapitated.

And with that, they were finished. They gave me back the magic marker and perfunctorily walked out the door. That was certainly an anticlimactic conclusion. I glanced down at the floor where the drawings of the decapitated snakes and frogs had unceremoniously been deposited, smiled encouragingly at Kwado, and hurriedly followed the would-be shamans out into the sunlight.

"Hey, Bakala, where did you learn how to perform that kind of healing? Who told you that was a good way to cure a rash?" I asked as we walked past the airstrip back toward my house.

He and Labeto stopped dead in their tracks and looked at me, surprise registering on their faces. "You don't know?" Bakala asked, stunned.

"I don't know. Tell me."

"That's what God's Talk tells us to do," he said, still not convinced that I really didn't know. After all, how could a missionary not know that this was what the Bible said to do?

Now it was my turn to be stunned. "Really?" was all I could manage to say.

Bakala, who had never read the Bible himself, went on to explain that the Bible describes how a bunch of people were dying from snake bites, and God told someone to make a snake, and then the people who had been bitten by the snakes were saved, and they didn't die.

OK. I was familiar with that biblical account, but I hadn't gotten the same thing out of it. The reality for Bakala and his people, however, was that, although they had heard little bits and pieces of Bible stories over the years from other tribal groups, they hadn't understood the stories in context. They had instead applied their own animistic thought process to the Bible, and as a result their animism was expanded to include rituals based very loosely on events in the Bible. This brought the added benefit, at least in their own minds, of following God's Talk, and having their animism endorsed by the God of the Bible. I suppose that was to be expected among a people who had never had God's Word in their own language.

We were hoping that would soon change. Both language learning and culture study were progressing well. It wouldn't be long before we could begin teaching the Bible to the Wilos, who for so long had been thirsting for it. I wondered what Bakala and Labeto would think about the account of Moses and the serpent in the wilderness once they understood it in the proper context.

Chapter 58

The Conundrum

How to keep the grub in my hand from winding up in my stomach

You would think that a comprehensive four-year missionary training course would include tips on how to avoid getting into tricky situations such as the one I was presently in, and also how to gracefully extricate yourself from them should you find yourself thus ensnared. As it was, I was burning up precious brain cells at a very rapid pace as my mind raced furiously in an effort to sort out all the options at my disposal and their possible ramifications.

Bruce, Joe and I had just survived a two-hour double-time hike through the jungle, around bogs, and over precarious bridges, following fast on the heels of the quickly moving Odowiya. I was relieved when he downshifted; we were arriving at Chelu's garden, where we would be visiting him and his family for a few hours.

We broke out into a large garden clearing, and Chelu and his daughter were standing on the trunk of a scorched fallen tree, looking out over their garden site much like a king and his royal princess might gaze down upon their kingdom.

We picked our way over fallen trees and around tree trunks and joined them on their perch. The hot sun was beating down, draining us of our remaining energy.

We had never been out to Chelu's garden before, and when he saw us, he was careful to extend all possible hospitality, which was why I found myself in such a delicate situation.

Immediately upon our arrival, Chelu had entered into an

animated conversation with Odowiya. Joe and Bruce were standing at the far end of the tree trunk, talking quietly together.

For my part, I was displaying great interest in a big white grub that had found its way into my hand, compliments of Chelu's daughter. I was not interested in the grub itself, but rather in ways to get the grub out of my hand in a tasteless yet gracious manner.

I knew that sometimes, something as simple as eating a grub can go a long way in developing good relationships with people who consider such things to be a delicacy. I thought of Bruce. He and his wife Cindy had joined our team of missionaries only a few short weeks before. They were new to Pakali, and had already dived into language and culture study.

Standing there amongst the shimmering heatwaves, looking at the grub in my hand, I suddenly had a spasm of inspiration. Wouldn't it be nice of me to pass along to my new co-worker Bruce this wonderful opportunity to bond with Chelu and his family? Something like this could really be a help to him and his acceptance into Wilo society.

True, by offering the grub to Bruce I would be passing up a great opportunity to further my own relationship with this Wilo family, but I was feeling magnanimous. Besides, I could work on developing relationships some other time, in some other way.

Grub in hand, I walked along the tree trunk to where Joe and Bruce were standing. "Hey, Bruce. Wanna try this?" I asked hopefully, extending the grub toward him. After all, you just never know what a new, enthusiastic missionary might be willing to do.

Bruce looked down at the grub and managed to pull off a vaguely pensive look, as though he were actually considering it. He then gave me a regretful shake of the head.

"No thanks," he said, in a tone suggesting that normally he would, but unfortunately he had just brushed his teeth.

Joe stood nearby, looking on apprehensively, but saying nothing. He and I had eaten a few grubs together on a previous occasion, back when we were new and enthusiastic missionaries, so I didn't even bother offering it to him. Instead, I just asked him to take a picture of it, which he did with much alacrity and relief.

With that, however, I had exhausted my repertoire of stalling tactics. I knew that the Wilo people were watching me out of the corners of their eyes. They would be greatly impressed were I to eat the grub. They had claimed on various occasions that doing so would help me learn to speak their language better.

My options had boiled down to these: I could eat the grub and thereby declare my solidarity with the Wilos, or I could put it back into the pan whence it came and run the risk of alienating the Wilos.

The grub was resting peacefully there in my hand, big, white, and no doubt excessively juicy. Looking down at it glumly, I could almost taste it, at least if the contractions in my stomach were any indication.

Deep inside I knew what I would have to do. All this posturing and pondering was merely postponing the inevitable. My mind was made up. There was really only one viable option; it was just a matter of mustering the courage and taking that first step.

Ready, one... two... three... In a single smooth motion I transferred the grub to my finger-tips, lifted it up, and... There, that wasn't so bad. A little distasteful, sure, but not nearly as distasteful as actually eating it.

Much to my relief, I saw that Chelu and his daughter were not offended in the least. They smiled, looking at the grub that once again rested in the pan, probably thinking, "All the more grubs for us." Chelu suggested we go to his house to get something to drink, which sounded good to me. Maybe we could all bond around a pot of hot fruit drink.

Chapter 59

Out and About with No Shorts

Tribal Bible lessons made easy

In my ongoing efforts to get out and about with the Wilo people and experience more of life as they know it, I wound up doing quite a bit with No Shorts. I would go hunting in the jungle with No Shorts. I would play soccer with No Shorts. I would go spearing fish, and I would go swimming with No Shorts. I would go visiting house to house with No Shorts. On occasion I would even spend days on end living out in the jungle with No Shorts. I would often sit at my table and drink coffee with No Shorts.

Getting out and about with No Shorts really helped me pick up a lot of Wilo language. Being with No Shorts helped me identify more with the Wilos; it helped me understand more of their culture and way of life. In short, No Shorts played a vital role in my ministry among the Wilos.

You would think being called "No Shorts" would create a hole in a person's psyche big enough to drive a truck through, but No Shorts displayed nothing but serenity about it all. I guess it's not such a bad name to have in a society where some people are named Diarrhea, and Vomit, and such.

Even No Shorts himself, otherwise known as Odowiya, was not quite sure how he came to be called this particular name, but he suspected it was because he used to run around without any clothes when he was a child. Well, yeah, that would make sense. But on second thought, with that reasoning, why wouldn't everybody in the entire village be called No Shorts?

No Shorts was a family man, a very big family man. In spite of his relative youth he had a dozen children of his own, and he showed no signs of cutting back his productivity, however much his weary but good-humored wife might have wished he do so.

Like practically every other Wilo, he was quick to smile, and slow to anger. He was a hard worker, clearing large garden sites where he and his family grew yucca, bananas, pineapple, papaya, and sugar-cane. When he wasn't at the garden he was usually off fishing. Keeping food on the table was a full-time job, even though technically, there was no table.

The thing that I appreciated the most about No Shorts, though, was his patience. I happened to be the grateful recipient of this patience of his on a regular basis. Even though, during the first couple of years in Pakali, I had not asked any of the Wilos to commit to being a daily language helper, I knew I would eventually have to. When that day came, I asked No Shorts if he would consider coming to my house every day to spend an hour or so helping me with language and culture study.

So every morning, five days a week, No Shorts would show up at my door. We would sit at the table, coffee mugs in hand, and he would help me learn to speak his language.

Over time, we developed an almost psychic ability to know what the other person was thinking. When I would start to say something and not know how to finish it, he would know what I was wanting to say and would finish my sentences for me. He got used to correcting the tiniest of details even when he could understand it the way I had said it. He developed an ability to absorb a lot of disjointed information from me and then organize it in his mind and give it back to me in a natural way that sounded wonderfully Wilo.

For my part, I learned to read his facial expressions and tonal inflections. I realized that No Shorts would almost never say outright that I had said something incorrectly. He would instead nod his head and then say, "Yeah, and you could say it *this* way as well," and then proceed to correct me. I learned to pay attention to his eyes. If he looked up when I was speaking, that usually meant he had heard me say something that wasn't quite right. If I kept pushing ahead without asking him what had caught his attention, he would just let it go and I would miss out on that opportunity to be corrected.

Those years of studying language with No Shorts did much to prepare the way for our team to begin developing the Bible lessons we would use to teach the Wilos. Not only was I gaining a fair degree of fluency in the Wilo language, but No Shorts and I were becoming familiar with how each other thought. I didn't know it at the time, but No Shorts would play a huge role in helping us develop effective Bible lessons that would communicate well the spiritual truths of the Bible.

Like many of the Wilos, No Shorts had heard bits and pieces of the gospel in the past, but never in his own language and never in a manner that took into account the unique culture of the Wilo people. What he and the others at Pakali had gleaned from it was anybody's guess.

Some of the Wilos had, at one point or another, professed to be Christians. In fact, when our missionary team first arrived, there was a mud-and-thatch building that served as a village church. On Sundays, many of the Wilos would attend services there and listen to the teachings that were presented in the language of the neighboring Owotojo tribe.

One night, a tropical storm passed through, and in the morning the church was lying flat; it had been reduced to a mound of leaves, rotted wood, and clay. It was never rebuilt, and soon after its collapse, the villagers who once had said they were Christians, decided they were Christians no more. How could they be, they often wondered aloud to us. After all, there was no church to attend anymore.

No Shorts, for his part, had told me that he definitely wasn't a Christian. But he and practically all of the other Wilos in the village continued to anxiously await the day when we would start teaching. And God was using No Shorts as a vital link in the process of assuring that he and his people would hear the Word of God in a clear and understandable way. His involvement in getting Bible lessons into his own language was what allowed us to eventually, after ten years of language and culture study, begin teaching the Bible to the Wilo people.

Chapter 60

The Dreaded Morning

The first day that the Wilo people heard Bible teaching in their own language

It was still dark outside. The roosters had been enthusiastically greeting the day since three o'clock that morning, so I decided I might as well get out of bed and do the same. Far from sharing the enthusiasm of the roosters, however, I was dreading the next few hours.

Our missionary team had been working toward this very day for the past ten years. I should have been thrilled. But no, I was too distracted to be thrilled: distracted with trying to undo the knots that had settled in the pit of my stomach.

Today was the day that the teaching of the Bible was to begin. That was exciting, and I would have been very upbeat about it all, but for one small detail: I was the one slated to do the teaching.

Why, you might wonder, would I leave my home country to live in an uncomfortable jungle, put up with hordes of biting insects, endure the constant stares and scrutiny of curious tribal people, spend ten long years learning an incredibly intricate tribal language, all in an effort to arrive at this day that I so dreaded?

That's exactly what I was wondering. It's not as though I didn't see it coming. I knew this day would arrive, and I had wanted it to arrive sooner than later. Now that it was actually here, though, I was extremely nervous. I kept an anxious eye on the clock, watching the minutes tick by.

The Wilos had decided that the meetings should be held at seven o'clock every morning, five days a week. The meeting house would be a storage shed: the same shed I had lived in many years ago when I first moved into the village.

Our missionary team had accomplished much over the course of the past ten years. We had attained a good degree of fluency in the language, although we still felt sadly inadequate to fully communicate the truths of the Bible. We had come to understand much about how the Wilo people viewed the world around them – both the physical world and the spiritual world. We had developed an alphabet for their language, and a good number of the villagers had already learned how to read and write in their own language; several of them in turn were now teaching others. We had begun translating scripture into their language.

Our team had undergone substantial personnel changes. Tim and Laurie had transferred to a different ministry in town, and Betilde had gotten married and was living out in town as well. Joe and Jackie had joined our team in 1996, and then Bruce and Cindy arrived in 2001. Marie came on board in 2002.

And now that most-awaited day had arrived. It was 23 September 2002, and seven o'clock was approaching all too quickly. It wasn't that we weren't prepared. Our team had spent countless hours developing the Bible lessons that would communicate clearly both to the ears and the minds of the Wilo people. We had mapped out a course that we intended to follow. Our team was ready for this, and the Wilos were anxious to hear. The weak link in the chain was the guy with knots in his stomach.

I picked up the binder that contained the lesson for that morning. I had gone over it dozens of times, but once more wouldn't hurt. It was a lesson that was primarily about the origins of the Bible: where it had come from and what it was.

I walked aimlessly from room to room, torn between wanting the hands on the clock to move faster or slower. I looked out the window and saw Joe walking past, toward the meeting house. It was still early, but I might as well go, too. I took a deep breath, prayed an anxious prayer and stepped out the door with Marie.

It was still rainy season, and a swarm of gnats followed as we made our way to the meeting house. We knew that many of the

Wilos who would begin hearing the teaching of God's Word that morning had serious misconceptions about the message. Some of them were expecting to hear a list of rules that they should adhere to in order to live a good and successful life. Others expected to receive instruction from the Bible about the best places to go fishing, when to work in the garden, and other such guidance on day-to-day decisions. Some thought the teaching of the Bible would be a retelling of their traditional myths and legends.

We hadn't attempted to correct these wrong assumptions; the Bible would speak for itself. What would the Wilos think when they realized that the Bible was about relationships, primarily that between God and man?

We saw little sign of normal village life that morning as we walked along. There were no gatherings of people in front of the houses discussing the day's plans. There were no women hanging clothes up to dry. The echoing sound of firewood being chopped was conspicuously absent. Had there been an exodus of people from the village yesterday? Had they forgotten that today was the day they had selected for the teaching to begin?

We rounded the corner of Kanem's house, and there was our answer. The villagers were already milling about in front of the meeting house, waiting for us to arrive. Ringing the bell to announce the beginning of the meeting was unnecessary, but we rang it nonetheless.

We all filtered into the store room. Some people sat on benches, others sat on the floor, and still others stood against the back wall. Outside, some of the villagers sat on their porches within hearing distance, and someone had climbed a nearby tree and was peering in from that vantage point. Nothing left but to begin speaking.

I don't remember anything about the meeting from that point on, but somehow, with the grace of a fish out of water, I got through it. The teaching of God's Word was underway.

Chapter 61

A Light in the Darkness

How will the Wilo people react when caught in the crosshairs of an angry witchdoctor?

Incidents of rape among the Wilo people were not common at all. They were not a violent society, and when someone acted out their anger they were usually reprimanded, or quickly, and at times mercilessly, ridiculed. Acts of excessive anger and violence were generally assumed to be antisocial, if not even perhaps a sign of the influence of evil spirits.

So when a little girl was violently raped, shockwaves reverberated through the village. This sort of thing was unheard of among them, unthinkable and unimaginable.

The girl was little more than a toddler. She had not yet learned to talk, and so could not identify the perpetrator of this awful crime.

In spite of the absence of eyewitnesses, the Wilos were quite certain about who the culprit was. Their suspect was an outsider from a neighboring tribe who happened to be visiting the village for a few days. He was staying with his older brother who worked as the government-sponsored medic for the region, and he had traded sharp words with the little girl's father not long before this crime was committed.

The crime was such that some military personnel came by river to investigate and take a report of the incident. By the time these people arrived, the Wilos had found the scene of the crime, and had been able to follow telltale footprints back toward the village for several hundred yards but no further.

The military people did what they could, but the lack of evidence pointing to a culprit prevented them from accomplishing anything of significance. They eventually returned to town, promising to follow up later.

The alleged culprit, meanwhile, had gone downriver to a village where his own people lived. Whether he was taking flight or simply reacting to the growing outrage against him wasn't clear. His older brother, however, remained and promptly engaged the Wilos in a war of words. Actually, it wasn't so much a war of words as it was a barrage of threats aimed at any Wilo person who dared point an accusing finger at his brother.

Was the medic threatening the Wilo people with physical harm? Was he threatening them with the suspension of medical help?

No, he was voicing a much more ominous threat. His father, you see, happened to be a powerful witchdoctor who apparently was chomping at the bit to unleash a flood of curses and hexes upon the hapless Wilo populace. If the Wilos didn't stop accusing this witchdoctor's son, he stood ready and willing to make them pay.

In the past, this type of threat had been employed with great success against the timid Wilo people. They had always been very fearful of being caught in the crosshairs of angry, vengeful witchdoctors, particularly those from other tribes.

Now though, things were a little different. Something else had been added to the mix, something called God's Talk.

One morning, while this battle of the wills was raging, Yanako came by our house to visit for a bit. As one of the village leaders, he was one of the primary targets of the threats coming from the medic and his witchdoctor father. He talked to us for a while about these threats against himself and his people. He concluded by shrugging dismissively and saying, "But we're not afraid."

Huh? "Really?" I prompted him for more explanation.

"That witchdoctor is a person, just like we are," he said. "He sits down and eats fish just like I do." Yanako then proceeded to mention many of the attributes of the God they had recently been learning about in the Bible. "God sees everything, all the time. God knows everything. Only God is all-powerful. God is the God of everybody.

"That witchdoctor," he continued, "didn't make the earth. He didn't make the stars in the sky. God sees everything that the witchdoctor does. God knows everything he is thinking. Only God is all-powerful. Nobody can hide from God."

He ended this line of thought by saying, "The medic's father has told us that he will cause snakes to bite us, and that other bad things will happen to us. But we're not afraid. He wants us to sink away from God's Talk and fear his witchcraft instead. That's why he threatens us. But we know that everyone dies. We will die, and the witchdoctor will die. Only God is eternal, and we want to learn more about him."

Does God's Word really have the power to effect change in people? This Wilo leader had yet to hear of Jesus Christ and the conclusion of the gospel story. However, in spite of the very limited amount of the Bible they had been able to hear up to this point, he and others of the Wilos were being changed. They were rethinking the traditional fears that for generations had held them in an unrelenting and unforgiving grip; they were being drawn instead toward freedom.

The little girl soon healed from the physical trauma of her experience; only time would tell what effects the emotional trauma would have on her life and development. Fortunately she was surrounded by people who were coming to view life through a biblical perspective. There was reason to hope that her people would come to view her through the biblical prism instead of stigmatizing her and branding her as a "no-good-one" for the rest of her life, as their culture would normally dictate. With God, after all, anything and everything is possible.

Chapter 62

Senior Citizens in Pakali

Two elderly village men listen to the Bible teaching with enthusiasm and wonderment

In the 1940s the world was embroiled in the turmoil and upheaval of World War II. Soldiers were fighting with guns. Airplanes were dropping bombs. Submarines were attacking from beneath the water's surface.

Meanwhile, in their little corner of the jungle, young Pelipe and Kalabu were ignorant of it all. Not only were they unaware of the war going on, they didn't even know there was a North America, a Europe, an Asia, an Africa, or even a South America. They were unfamiliar with guns; they didn't know what airplanes were. And submarines? Well, that was just a ridiculous concept. Their world was very small indeed. They were attempting merely to survive the hardships of jungle life.

While much of the world was living in fear of nuclear winter during the cold war, Pelipe and Kalabu, now middle-aged, were oblivious to that, as well. They had their own fears to deal with: fear of the evil spirits, fear of the witchdoctors, and fear of the many spiritual dangers in the world around them.

And while many of us were reluctantly trudging to church on Sunday mornings, lamenting the fact that we had to listen to yet another sermon, Pelipe and Kalabu could only hope that one day they would be able to hear even just a little of God's Word.

Pelipe and Kalabu were the two oldest men in the village. They were old when we first arrived in Pakali in 1992. We often prayed that God would preserve their lives so they would be able to hear

210

God's Word in their own language. They had wanted that for many years; it would be terrible if they were to die before we could learn their language and teach the Bible clearly. We were so thankful to see that, as the years went by, these two senior citizens maintained their health and changed very little.

Pelipe lived several houses down from Kalabu. He presented something of a scandal in the village because he had fathered children with his own daughter. He was quite blind, as well as being hard of hearing, and the volume on his voice-box seemed to be stuck on "high".

But in spite of his physical limitations, he remained fairly independent and relatively active, which was a good thing because, while the Wilos don't denigrate old people, neither do they highly esteem them nor think to always look out for their well-being.

Kalabu, unlike Pelipe, was something of a house hermit. His wild, white mane of hair and a small bamboo shoot occupying a hole pierced in his lower lip gave him a distinctive look. He was the Wilo that was said to know the most about witchcraft. Unlike his neighbor and contemporary Pelipe, Kalabu was possessed of all his senses, but he was rather frail, and much less adventurous than his blind friend.

We rarely saw either of them, unless we stopped by their houses to visit. But once the teaching of the Bible began, they would every day come to the teaching sessions together. Even before the clanging bell announced that the morning meeting would soon be getting underway, they could often be seen making their way through the village, with Pelipe, blind but determined, cautiously leading the frail Kalabu to the meeting house.

Once inside the meeting room, they would be led to their reserved seating right under one of the stereo speakers. They would sit up against the side wall, and as the teaching was presented, their excited comments, pensive grunts, and enthusiastic feedback would reverberate throughout the building, sometimes with such volume that everybody would turn to look at them. Pelipe especially was fond of shouting under his breath,

211

"Would you listen to that!" whenever something struck him as exceptional.

On those afternoons when recorded review lessons were being replayed on the rustic sound system at the meeting house, Pelipe and Kalabu were usually there, seated in the same spot. Listening to recordings was something new to these two elderly Wilos. They interacted with the disembodied voice of the recording much like they did at the morning meetings, answering questions, mumbling to each other, and every now and then exclaiming, "Would you listen to that!"

They, as well as many of the other Wilos, seemed to be hearing much more than the voice of the messengers. They were not only hearing the words, but were convinced the Bible held the answers they had so desperately been waiting for. It was as though God's Spirit, by means of the Bible, was taking them on a tour of who God is and how he interacts with man. With each new truth presented, they were stunned anew and often in unison would blurt it out again: "Would you listen to that!" The light of God's Word was penetrating the darkness that had been their spiritual reality, and they were loving it.

Chapter 63

The Redeemer is Born

After many months of teaching from the Old Testament, Jesus Christ is introduced to the Wilos

By this time we had taught for several months, covering material about the creation of the earth, about Adam and Eve, Cain and Abel, Noah and the flood, the tower of Babel, the life of Abraham, the emergence of the nation of Israel, Joseph being sold into slavery, Israel's captivity in Egypt, their eventual exodus from Egypt and the subsequent wanderings in the wilderness.

No Shorts and I continued working feverishly on getting more Bible lessons into the Wilo language. With teaching roughly an hour a day for five days a week, we were going through the material faster than we were able to develop new stuff, and our original buffer of prepared teaching lessons was shrinking all too quickly.

We continued teaching about Israel, and their entrance into the promised land of Canaan. We focused often on God's recurring promise to one day send a Redeemer who would pay the penalty of sin once and for all. We taught on the many prophecies of the coming Messiah. Would God's promises and these prophecies actually come true? Would God provide a way for sinful man to come back into a perfect relationship with himself?

Finally, after spending five months teaching from the Old Testament, we began teaching about Jesus. We referred back to the prophecies regarding the birth of the Messiah; Jesus was a perfect fit. The Wilos loved seeing how the promises and prophecies from the Old Testament were being fulfilled one after another as they learned more and more about the life of Jesus. There was no doubt in their minds that the promised Redeemer had made his appearance.

They identified with the system of works and outward appearances that many Jewish leaders of the day adhered to. The words that Jesus spoke against that system spoke directly to the Wilos' own hearts. They were struck time and time again by the fact that God looks on the inside, while man looks only on the outside. God would be satisfied with nothing less than complete inward cleanliness.

When they learned that John the Baptist called Jesus the Lamb of God, even though most of them had never seen a real lamb before, they knew exactly what John was referring to and what he was implying, because through the previous months of teaching they had already learned about the Old Testament system of sacrifices.

The many miracles that Jesus performed were proof to many Wilos that the message Jesus spoke was a message directly from God. The humility that Jesus showed was contrary to their own culture of gossip and judgmentalism, much like it is contrary to our own culture of seeking our own good, our own status and esteem.

When the Wilos heard the parable of the person who went out to sow seeds, they excitedly gathered together after the meeting to talk about it.

"We used to be just like the hard ground that didn't allow the seeds to penetrate and put down roots, but now that we're hearing God's Talk in our own language and understanding it, God's Spirit is causing the seeds to grow," Lati said, a dawning comprehension bringing excitement to his voice.

Well before the teaching had begun, the Wilos had viewed the Bible as a spiritual authority, and they yearned for it. We hadn't needed to convince them to take God's Talk seriously. This conviction of theirs seemed to stem from their own growing sense of disillusionment and dissatisfaction with what for generations had been the only belief system available to them. They had been subjected since early childhood to the fears and superstitions that underlay their traditional beliefs. The Bible's message was different; it was bringing hope and freedom into their world, and they were reveling in it.

And then Palo died.

Chapter 64

A Death in the Village

How will a sudden and shocking death affect the villagers?

Palo was a young teenager when we first arrived in Pakali. His house was not far from ours, and he loved spending time with us strange people. He was inquisitive and had a tremendous desire to learn as much as he could about the outside world. We provided his best source for that kind of information. He spoke a bit of Spanish, which allowed him to communicate with us, at least on a very superficial level, right from day one.

He was attending the government school in Pakali but, like all the Wilo children who attended that school, he wasn't learning much. None of the teachers spoke his language, so he was limited in what he was able to glean from the classes.

But he stuck with it, eventually even leaving Pakali to pursue further schooling at an outpost several days' travel downriver. His motivation propelled him into the unique position of being one of the best-schooled Wilo people ever. He learned to read and write in Spanish, and once we had developed an alphabet for his own language it took him little time to become literate in that as well. He was good at math, and enjoyed teaching others.

He also began getting involved in local politics. The national government was encouraging all tribal people to form committees and appoint representatives who could serve as a link between the tribe and the government. Palo was ideal for that kind of work.

He continued spending a lot of time with us missionaries, helping with language learning and culture study. He also helped us as we began translating portions of the Bible into his language.

He was a hard worker and in spite of the many other things he was involved in, he never neglected to work at his garden and provide for his family by fishing and hunting along with everybody else. He was a great athlete and would organize *futbol* and *futbolito* tournaments with other villages, getting out the invitations and working on the logistics.

And as if that wasn't enough, he eventually began working as a substitute teacher at the government school in Pakali. Palo, as you might have already noted, was a big part of the Pakali society. A few other young people of his generation were following the same path, pursuing education outside of the village, and getting involved in politics, but no one did so with more grace and maturity than Palo.

He was full of promise – the promise of living a full life, and having a tremendous influence on the progress and well-being of his people. As we witnessed God's Word having an impact in his own life, we wondered if Palo might not become a spiritual leader as well.

He rarely missed the morning Bible teaching sessions. Even when he had to be at his teacher's post at the school by eight o'clock, he would stay in the meeting room as long as possible. He was part of the group that would sit at a table at the front of the room while the Bible lesson was being taught.

His father, on the other hand, rarely came to the meetings. He had always been friendly to us, and remained so, but he wasn't at all interested in learning about the message of the Bible. He dabbled in witchcraft and preferred to follow the animistic beliefs of his forefathers. Of all the people in the village, Palo's father seemed the least interested in the Bible.

One morning Palo decided to join in a game of *futbol* with a few children. He had barely stepped onto the pitch when he collapsed to the ground, unconscious. A few adults who happened to be standing nearby carried him to his house and laid him in his hammock. They believed he had simply over-exerted himself and had fainted due to the heat. While some of them fanned him, a few others came to our door to tell us what had happened.

Marie went to Palo's house with them. There was a group of people crowded around him. A few of them said they could feel his pulse and they were confident he would soon revive. Checking Palo for a pulse, she had found no response, but the Wilos insisted he had simply fainted. After standing around for a while, Marie came home. She was concerned for Palo; she felt he was in a serious condition.

The sound of people approaching our door just a few minutes later made our hearts sink. The two ladies were crying and saying that we should come right away. We went back to Palo's house with them and entered a room where several people were quietly crying. Palo was still in his hammock, and people were fanning him with mats woven from palm leaves. Trying for a pulse, we again found nothing.

We took him out of the hammock and placed him on the ground. We attempted to revive him by performing mouth-to-mouth resuscitation for a minute or two, but we could tell he was already dead. We were all devastated.

Because he had been a member of the local political body, the government provided a casket for his burial and we buried him in the cemetery on a small hill out beyond the airstrip.

A sudden, inexplicable death like Palo's would have normally sent the Wilos into panic and fear as they attempted to figure out why a witchdoctor or the evil spirits would have wanted him dead. They would have speculated about who was going to die next. They would have agonized over what they should do to prevent further deaths in their village.

In the case of Palo, though, what we heard people saying was, "Only God knows." They seemed content to leave the situation in God's hands.

A few people clipped off pieces of Palo's fingernails and hair before he was buried, and they took those clippings upriver to a witchdoctor to see if he might be able to shed some light on why Palo had died. We weren't surprised that some of them would do this. What *did* surprise us, though, was the response of the witchdoctor. He reprimanded them, saying that they were now people who had God's Word; they shouldn't be resorting to divinations and witchcraft.

We had taught through most of the life of Christ, and had been on the verge of teaching about his betrayal and arrest. We knew that Palo had been listening carefully to the teaching, but he had never told us that he was actually believing God's Word and trusting in the Redeemer. His widow, however, told us not long after, that Palo had told her that he was indeed trusting that the Redeemer would pay the debt of his sin.

Palo was buried on a Saturday, and on Monday we continued the teaching. We didn't know how Palo's death would affect the rest of the Wilos. Would they withdraw from the teaching, thinking that perhaps the spirits were punishing them for listening to the Bible? Would they feel antagonistic toward God? We didn't know how things would proceed.

We got to the meeting house, and many people were already there, some seated inside, others standing around outside waiting for the teaching to get underway. I shouldn't have been surprised, but I admit I was. I had once again underestimated the life-changing power of God's Spirit in the hearts and minds of people who are believing him and trusting him. Palo's death wasn't putting fear into their hearts. Rather, it seemed to be highlighting in their minds the hope of eternal life.

When I stepped into the meeting room, an even larger surprise awaited me. Standing against the back wall was Palo's father. His sadness and pain were visible on his face. I didn't know what exactly had brought him to the meeting, but I was happy to see him there, as were the others. He rarely missed a meeting from that day on.

Chapter 65

In Their Own Words

The Wilo people express their thoughts regarding God's Talk

We spent the next couple of weeks teaching through the account of Christ's betrayal, his arrest, the abuse he suffered, his death, his burial, and his resurrection. We were nearing the conclusion of the gospel story, but we didn't really know how we should handle the final day of teaching. After ten months of communicating God's life-giving truths to the Wilos, what would be the culturally appropriate way to conclude such an important message?

We decided we would simply open up the meeting for people to say anything at all about the teaching. So, when we finished teaching about Christ's resurrection from the dead, we gave an invitation. It was an invitation, not for them to come forward to receive Christ as their Savior, but simply an invitation for them to address the group regarding what they thought about God's Talk.

Knowing how timid the Wilos generally are, we didn't know if anyone would have the inclination and the fortitude to speak publicly. We had no idea what to expect. We had just spent several days looking out over a large but somber and sad group of Wilo listeners as we taught about Christ's betrayal, trial, and crucifixion. And we had seen that sadness dissipate and give way to bright smiles as we taught about the resurrection of Christ from the dead. After months of us doing the talking, we wanted to give them an opportunity to express in a public forum what they were thinking. We sat down.

Before I was able to even fully take the weight off of my feet,

Bayuli, a young married man, stood up and began speaking. This is what he said:

"We've heard God's Talk for several months now. We used to think we were clean on the inside, but we've heard now that the Redeemer paid for our sins. Only if we rest our souls on the Redeemer will we arrive to God, because he paid for our sins. Because our grandfather Adam, having been created by God, separated himself from God and went with Satan, we also were all born on Satan's trail. We were born as captives, just like Adam and Eve became captive and weren't able to return to God's trail on their own.

"And Abraham was commanded by God to kill his own son, and when he was on the verge of doing so, God provided a lamb and he sacrificed the lamb and his son was saved. God, who made all animals, provided the lamb that Abraham killed and sacrificed.

"And we heard how God gave his own Son Jesus, who came as a lamb of God to pay for our sins. What does that mean for us? Just like God provided the lamb for Isaac to be saved, so Jesus came to redeem us, hanging on a tree.

"And when Nicodemus came to talk to Jesus and asked how to be saved, Jesus told him he needed to be born again. Nicodemus said, 'How can I, being grown, be born again?' Jesus told Nicodemus that he needed to be born again by God. Jesus said that only if he rested his soul on the Redeemer who would be lifted up on a pole could he be saved. And Jesus said that he would die and would be dead for only three days and would rise again. And it happened just like he said, because he is God.

"Jesus was talking to Nicodemus about himself, about his future death on the cross, so that Nicodemus would know."

Bayuli talked about Abraham and Isaac, and about the significance of John the Baptist referring to Jesus as the Lamb of God. Just when I was beginning to wonder if I should have brought a cushion, Bayuli finished with this simple statement:

"And for us there remains nothing else. We've heard all of this. The only way for us to be saved is to trust in the Redeemer."

Welcome to eternal life, Bayuli.

After him came a steady stream of people, men and women, young and old. I did need that cushion after all. We sat for two hours listening as dozens of people publicly expressed, in their own way and with their own words, that their sin could only be paid for by the Redeemer sent by God, and that they were giving their sin to Jesus Christ, the one who died to pay for it all.

Yanako, the captain of the village, stood to say this: "We've heard about the words of salvation. We've heard about how Adam and Eve separated from God. We've learned that the Redeemer came to pay the price of our sin. We are all born as sinners, because we are born from Adam. Because we have sin, Jesus, who had no sin, came and died to pay the debt of our sin. If we wish to go on God's trail, we must trust in the Redeemer. I have no strength to arrive to God on my own. Only God is all-powerful. I am trusting in the Redeemer, and will continue on with him."

Jelema had this to say: "I will say a bit for myself. I know, from having heard all these things from God's Talk, that we have no strength to get to God on our own. Only God has no sin. Only if I trust in God can I arrive. Only God has no sin, and I am resting my soul on him. We should all trust in the Redeemer and give to him the sin that we have."

Lama referred back to the account of the bronze serpent that was made by Moses and placed up on a pole. He said, "Just like the people of Israel were able to look at that serpent and be saved from the snakes, in that same way I am looking at the Redeemer to pay the debt of death that I have before God."

I sat on a little wooden bench listening to these words, and was struck by my own inner response to what was unfolding before my eyes. I would have expected to feel elated, euphoric even, and yet I felt strangely subdued. I was very aware of the fact that no amount of human effort could have produced this kind of spiritual fruit. It was God who had been at work all these years – at work both in me, and in the Wilo people.

Did all the Wilos profess faith in Christ that day? No. In fact, a prominent woman of the village stood up to tell everybody that she still did not believe. She didn't say it defensively, nor was she antagonistic. But with simplicity and honesty she let everyone know what was in her heart. Many in the room murmured their approval of her comments, including us missionaries.

One young man concluded his talk by turning to us and saying, "The things that we are saying today are not things that you have taught us; they are things that God's Spirit has taught our spirit."

I was never more happy to be rendered irrelevant. The messengers were set aside now that direct communication had been established.

Chapter 66

Two Wars – Different but the Same

While the war in Iraq raged, a spiritual war was underway in the Amazon jungle

If you were anywhere in the vicinity of a television in April of the year 2003, you probably saw images of American forces and Iraqi civilians pulling down a huge statue of Saddam Hussein. It was a largely symbolic act, and was one of the defining moments of the war in Iraq. It was meaningful not because pulling down the statue gave the Iraqis their freedom; it didn't. It was meaningful because it symbolized the freedom that they had obtained. One Iraqi who participated said that it made him feel born again.

For those Iraqis it symbolized the end of decades of oppression, and for the coalition forces it was an indication that, after all the planning, months of preparation, and several weeks of open battle, freedom had finally come to the Iraqi people. The celebration and jubilation of that small group of Iraqis testified to the relief and delight the Iraqis felt at having been liberated from years of tyranny, torture, intimidation and insignificance. They had passed from oppression to freedom, from fear to liberty. So, they helped tear down the statue that symbolized the hated past.

And then what? Did freedom flourish? Did peace reign? Did coalition forces withdraw? Was it "mission accomplished"? Did the Iraqi people bask in their new-found freedom and set a united course toward democracy, peace, and prosperity?

No, not exactly. The statue came down, and the long, difficult, and very complicated process of walking in that freedom began. Freedom had been attained, but learning how to live in that freedom was to be an ongoing endeavor. The Iraqis had been liberated from an obvious and arrogant tyrant, but other, more subtle tyrants were waiting in the wings, wishing to envelop the nation of Iraq in a cocoon of cruel oppression yet again.

Meanwhile, on a completely unrelated front, a spiritual battle had been taking place on the opposite side of the world where an entrenched tyrant was doing what he could to repel the approaching freedom that was challenging his dominion.

The battlefield was a small, unassuming village in the middle of the jungle. The battle had been enjoined in the hope of bringing spiritual light and freedom to the Wilo people. The Wilos had, for decades, desired to hear God's Word. After roughly twenty-five years of asking for missionaries, and then ten years more of helping the missionaries learn their language and culture, the Wilos were finally hearing God's Word in their own language for the very first time.

There were no statues to topple, and no streets in which to celebrate. Instead, the defining moment for the Wilos came when many of them gave clear testimony of their belief and trust in the gospel of Christ. This public testimony obviously did not give them spiritual freedom; it merely expressed the freedom that had finally come to them. After generations of spiritual darkness and slavery to sin, God's Word had brought light and freedom to the Wilos.

So, what was next for us missionaries? Was that it? Did we pack our bags and go home, expecting the Wilos to know how to walk in their new-found freedom?

No, not exactly. True, the tyrant had been exposed. Now the focus shifted to seeing the Wilo believers established in God's Word. The road to maturity is anything but short and simple. Pitfalls and distractions complicate the way. Fortunately, the Bible very clearly explains not only the way to freedom, but also how to live and grow in that freedom.

Thousands of people the world over had joined in prayer, and in giving, and in helping in many different ways. As a result, a people who had for generations been longing to hear God's Word, had finally been able to do so.

Long ago a man named Ezekiel wrote about life coming to a valley of bones. Thousands of years after Ezekiel's death a young Wilo man named Bitimi wrote this about life coming to his own valley:

A while ago I heard God's Talk and came to understand.
I came to understand that I was living separated from my Lord God because I have sin.
I came to understand this because God's Talk says it clearly.

He was not unwilling. He wanted to.
He himself paid the debt for all of my sin. He erased it away.
I arrived on God's trail that day because Jesus paid the debt of my sin. I was born again on that day.
Now I am not a slave of Satan. I am a child of God. I am the brother of Jesus.
On that day I became a child of God.
Now I live in peace.
Knowing that when I die, I will go to live with God, I live in peace, without fear.

Made in the USA
San Bernardino, CA
15 June 2020